PERMITTED FRUIT

A HEALING INTUITIVE EATING TRANSFORMATION

Heather Mitchell

Join our Facebook group to discuss your journey with me and others.
@ www.facebook.com/groups/PermittedFruit

Follow Heather on Instagram

@Permitted.Fruit

Plentifold Publishing

www.plentifold.com

For all the support to Anna & Jan

"Divide each difficulty into as many parts as is feasible and necessary to resolve it, and watch the whole transform." – Rene Descartes

TABLE OF CONTENTS

FOREWORD

Did you know that, even with the thousands of diets we are bombarded with over our lifetime, we have an instinct that tells us what we should eat? Did you know that eating does not even have to be an issue at all actually, on the contrary, it should be a pleasant experience? The instinct is real, you just have to develop and exercise it. It's called Intuitive Eating and it's what nutritional therapist and diet expert Heather Mitchell tells us in this reading through her own experience as well as those of the people she worked with.

Heather went from maintaining a toxic relationship with food for a large part of her life to finding her intuitive eater and managed to create a harmonious relationship with her diet in which she's able to be attuned to her body and achieve the results she desires, without extreme restrictions which generally lead to frustrating, perpetual cycles of losing and gaining weight. In the same way she has helped many men and women to better understand their eating process, greatly decreasing their anxiety about hunger or food and respecting their physiognomy.

Over the years we've been surrounded by food restrictions and it seems that every decade has some food to condemn. In the 90s the prohibition was on carbohydrates, at the beginning of 2000 it was sugar and fat, now they are dairy and gluten. We see all kind of diets: without meat, with restriction of fruit, diets without carbohydrates, with strict schedules for particular kind of foods, diets in which the fact of staying hungry is justified as if it were some kind of feat. Endless possibilities that leads us to think that, in the end, we rely more on a generic diet, written on a random paper, than on our own instincts. We believe we know what healthy foods are only because of what society has taught us, without thinking about our nutrition, which has generated a high percentage of obsessive disorders around foods such as orthorexia (the unhealthy obsession with eating healthily) even in health professionals.

One of the concepts that Heather seeks to clarify in this guide is emotional eating and how to recognize those moments of anxiety, sadness, loneliness, anger, boredom, emotion or nervousness in which we can spend days with great willpower until eventually, we succumb to excesses like overeating, binge eating or use food as a method of therapy causing the same effect. It´s important to know that emotional eating is comforting at first, the problem is that it does not solve any of the situations we were facing. It becomes a distraction from reality and in the long run, these excesses only fill us with guilt and resentment against ourselves, ending up demonizing food.

If you start this book feeling skeptical of what you'll read, that is perfectly normal. However, as a health professional, I can assure you that you will quickly realize that it is not another diet book. Rather, it will change your way of thinking about food that will lead you to eat "what you want when you need it" instead of "what you can when you should". In addition to developing mental awareness and to stay alert to the signals of our bodies, it will also be a manual to learn and enjoy physical activity without obsessing about exercising to "win" the "forbidden" foods as a reward. Exercise should be a generator of positive experiences, a way to create well-being from moving your body and not a type of military training to burn calories. Once we manage to accept our body image realistically as a blue print, the perfect figure imposed on us will cease to be important and we will achieve peace of mind. With a body that is perfectly summarized in that basic roman concept dating from the 2nd century of which Heather is a faithful believer: mens sana in corpore sano (a healthy mind in a healthy body), knowing one cannot be achieved without the other. From there, growing an awareness of the toxic diet culture that surrounds us, accepting our own body and reconnecting with it, should be the common sense way forward. Attentive to which signals are being sent to our brain, understanding the body as a whole and not as individual parts that work on their own.

Body re-connection begins by accepting normal physiological processes and not trying to suppress feelings that are totally normal, which is what we do when we feel guilty for being hungry. Depriving us of food in times of hunger leads to dangerous excesses that not only have aesthetic repercussions but also biochemical, dangerously raising or lowering levels of sugar, proteins, cholesterol and triglycerides which can trigger metabolic diseases. The intuitive eater manages to satisfy the nutritional needs of the present without condemning any food nor any normal physiological process. We eat if we are hungry but are aware of our level of hunger and satiety at all times which will, over time, become much easier to identify. Intuitive eating takes us one step further in the general understanding of a diet. It gives us the opportunity to take responsibility for our own health and to become aware that food is part of an internal natural process that is reflected in our body image.

This book represents a journey that goes beyond a diet or a nutritional guide. Throughout the reading we'll learn by the experiences of Heather, which are recognizable to most of us, how to give meaning to the events that lead us maintaining a poor diet and health in the first place. Physiological processes do not stop but by making our mind and the way in which we nourish ourselves an active part of our diet, we will not only create a better relationship with food but also with our body resulting in better health. When you finish this book you can make peace with yourself and with the food you eat. Get ready to start walking down that road.

Maybell Nieves M.D.

INTRODUCTION

There are a large number of books out there when it comes to the topic of dieting and eating right. Everything from cookbooks to meal plans to highly scientific diet books, all of which promise the same thing: Start eating right and lose weight fast.

Now, I have no idea how many diets you've tried thus far. What I do know is, if you've picked up this book, you're sick and tired of the promises and the claims that those other books make. You're probably in the same position as I was in the not too distant past, frustrated at my lack of progress and desperately seeking something which would work.

The truth is that most diets fail. This is something we all know and have experience with. How many of us truly know *why* they fail though? Why do diets seem to work theoretically but fall apart practically? This book is going to give you that answer, and in the process, you will understand why your diet plans and weight loss

5

goals have not been achieved.

Intuitive eating is nothing short of revolutionary when it comes to gaining the body you want. Along the way, not only will your body thank you for adopting this easy to follow, no gimmicks eating pattern, your mind will be so much more at ease and relaxed.

In short, intuitive eating is a balm, not just for your body, but for your mind as well.

THE DIFFERENCE

All diets -be it the Ketogenic diet, Paleo, South Beach, Atkins, you name it- have one thing in common which guarantees they will fail. They all ignore the effect the diet has on the mind. I vividly recall the excitement of discovering a new diet and starting a diet plan.

For the first few weeks everything would be fine but soon after, inexplicably, my brain would begin to refuse to follow the diet's instructions. In vain, I would turn to books and online blogs for help, just to be told "You need to be mentally strong!" as if that was all it took! I would knuckle down and tell myself to commit to the diet, all the while putting myself under unbearable strain, and forcing myself to eat the food I was supposed to.

How many of you can relate to the above? You see, following diets in this manner only damages your relationship with food. You look at the food you used to love with a jaundiced eye and bounce between starving yourself or binge eating. I know I did! In my case, the excessive guilt and stress it would build up would result in the cheat day morphing into a cheat week!

I never did understand why this would happen. After all, I am a well-adjusted person in all other areas. Why was my brain and body revolting like this to my efforts to get healthier? I began to view them as traitors, which needless to say, is the worst possible thing you can say to yourself.

With my self image at rock bottom, hating myself every time I looked into a mirror, I eventually decided enough was enough. The first step to health and well being is to love yourself. I decided to consciously practice this and forgot about the dieting plans for a while. Anything that caused me stress or caused me to hate myself had no more place in my life!

Soon, with my mind in a much better and more accepting place, I began to apply the same principles to my eating habits. Just like magic, I began to look and feel healthier! I don't mean healthier from just a self-acceptance standpoint but also a physical one! I used to religiously measure myself when I was following my old diets and was always met with frustration.

Now, by some miracle, I was easily making progress, looking healthier and feeling wonderful too! I was not starving myself or following some complicated macro calculation strategy. What was going on?

This is how I discovered the process of intuitive eating and the importance of listening to your body and mind. Intuitive eating has a set of core principles which will help you blow past any old beliefs and issues which hamper you. We will examine these principles in detail and also give you actionable steps to practice this in your daily lives.

Intuitive eating is not just a diet plan for me. It is a way of life. It has rescued me from the depths of self-hatred and taught me to apply self-love and acceptance, along with mindfulness, to my eating habits. I consider it my mission to help as many people as possible who are stuck in the vicious cycle that the pressure to live up to an ideal image brings.

There is no ideal image. You are wonderful as you are and do not need to change a thing except following the right path. The light at the end of the tunnel is a lot closer than you think!

So let's step together into the world on intuitive eating and explore how you can change your life by just practicing a few simple steps. If you feel like sharing your thoughts on this book, I kindly ask you to leave a review on Amazon or Audible. It would help me spread the word and help more people.

One more thing before we begin... How would you like to continue listening to this book during that morning rush hour commute with your hands free?

Enter the **Audiobook!** Best Of All, it's **Free!**

With a trial of the Audible subscription.

Bonus: you get another book free as well when you sign up.

Visit plentifold.com to receive your free copy.

THE BEGINNING OF THE END

Show of hands, how many of you have tried all the fancy diets out there? How many of you have eaten super foods only to end up super fat? How many of you have had that clean, lean, detox, calorie reduced, guilt-free chocolate, avocado smoothie (yuck!) only to feel the need to eat some real food right after?

Why is our relationship to food so fraught? Why can't we just eat like a normal person? Well, therein lies the problem. What's normal these days is anything but.

Image Obsession

A regular morning ritual for most of us after waking up, is to scroll over our social media feeds and catch up on things. Social media is a wonderful tool and brings us closer together. However, it also has an unintentional side effect of causing us to compare ourselves to our friends and others we're linked to.

Those wonderful vacation photos in that exotic locale your friend and her family went on, are now a yardstick to match instead of being something to get excited about. Social media has injected the phenomenon of "keeping up with the Joneses" and turned into a full-blown geared out monster!

Look, comparing yourself to another person has its benefits. By looking at the other person's achievements we can inspire ourselves to greater heights and push ourselves to extremes we wouldn't have even dreamed of otherwise. I mean, consider the 4-minute mile. What Roger Bannister achieved in 1954 was thought to be impossible. Well, do you know that by 1990, the New Zealander Sir John George Walker, had run a sub 4-minute mile 135 times?

Did something inherently change in athletics that within the space of 40 years, something impossible that began to be considered routine? You bet! It was the mindset with which runners approached the track! You see, our brains are wonderful things which can help us achieve anything we set our heart's desire upon.

What does all this have to do with dieting, you might be asking. Well, today's age of social media has taken the ways our minds seek inspiration and bombarded them with completely unrealistic images and 2a warped definition of normal. Our Instagram feeds are loaded with images of women who are impossibly thin, travel the world, hang out on beaches sipping Pina Coladas all the time, and have the most fun-filled, exciting lives ever! All of that seems a far cry from our disheveled selves, in crumpled pajamas, and unruly hair wondering how many loads of laundry it's going to take to get all the washing done.

This negative state of mind that gets impressed upon us affects every aspect of our lives. What car does that irresistibly sexy model drive? A Mercedes? Well, I drive a Kia. How often does she workout? Always? Well, I workout "just" 5 hours a week. What food does she eat? Only vegan food? Well, I gorge myself on meat, potatoes, chocolate cake and wine all the time! What is wrong with me!? How did I ever get this far off course?!

Thus begins the messed up relationship we have with food. Suddenly, that succulent piece of meat becomes the Antichrist and chocolate cakes might as well be fed to your enemies (oh, you don't have those either? How boring!)

HOW DIET DISORDERS BEGIN

This extremely unrealistic view of what is ideal leads us to adopt diets and constantly beating ourselves up over how we look, feel and act. The entire point of a diet is that it's supposed to make you healthy. However, all of this is forgotten in the face of those selfies and swimsuit pics on your Instagram feed.

Given the unrealistic expectations people begin with, it's only normal that the diets will fail. Our bodies are fundamentally designed to stay healthy. How is placing restrictions on it and cutting off certain vital food groups according to some diet, keeping it healthy? Naturally, our bodies will revolt!

This leads to the all too familiar up and down fluctuation of body weight. We press and press with our diets and our weight drops. Our bodies revolt to this unnatural sensation and rushes back to equilibrium, with weight gain being an added bonus.

Instead of heeding these cues, most people will double and triple down on their diets and eventually, under the weight of the stress placed on it, the body simply succumbs to eating disorders and disease. How many of you have heard of the below diseases?

- Anorexia Nervosa

- Bulimia Nervosa

- Purging

- Avoidant food intake disorder

- Pica

- Rumination Syndrome

- Orthorexia

- Night eating syndrome

- Diabulimia

Ask yourself, why do you even know of these disorders? Why has our culture gotten to the point where almost everyone is aware of someone or the other who suffers from these diseases? Is this the sign of a healthy culture? After all, the person who suffers from disease knows the names of all the medications and disorders more than the healthy person does. This doesn't mean to say that just because you know the name of the disorder, you must be suffering from it. What I'm trying to get across is that our culture these days is completely poisoned when it comes to our relationship with food. What is meant to nourish us has become the enemy.

The Cure

The cure for all this begins with carrying out a reset of our mind's attitudes when it comes to food and nutrition. You see, it's time to start trusting ourselves again. We're more than equipped to know what's good or bad for us and we don't need some influencer or social media start telling us what to do and what to eat.

It is time all of us plugged ourselves out of this mess and revisit the basics. When someone suffers from an addiction, an intervention is often carried out by those closest to the addict. Whether you care to accept it or not, you have been forced into an addiction of sorts when it comes to your eating habits and the way you view food.

Consider me your best friend and the rest of this book as your intervention.

Great news!

You can receive "Permitted Fruit Food Journal"

For Free
This printable diary can motivate you in difficult moments, support you by seeing past accomplishments, and help track your journey towards a mindful way of enjoying food.

Simply go to **www.plentifold.com/intuitivediary** to receive it right away.

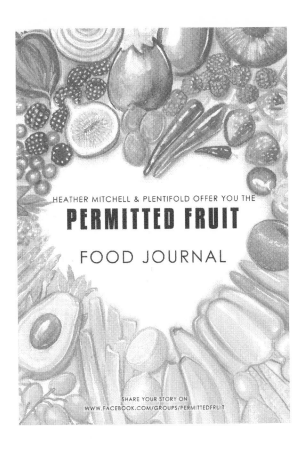

HEATHER MITCHELL & PLENTIFOLD OFFER YOU THE
PERMITTED FRUIT
FOOD JOURNAL

SHARE YOUR STORY ON
WWW.FACEBOOK.COM/GROUPS/PERMITTEDFRUIT

STEP 1- DIET CULTURE: UNSUBSCRIBE NOW!

So are you excited yet? You should be! You're on the verge of beginning to finally eat the right way, the way you're supposed to as nature intended.

This chapter will give you the lowdown on how dieting affects your body and the steps you can take to get rid of this toxic habit and the associated thought patterns forever.

So let's dive in and explore this further!

The Dieting Lie

Somewhere towards the end of the previous century, as TV and mass media proliferation became greater than ever before, an ad executive must have had a wonderful idea. All advertising is created with the intent of enforcing scarcity. Buy this now or you'll never measure up! This offer will last for just two more seconds!

Why not take this principle and apply it to the way we eat? Why not sell eating as a special tool to get fit? After all, the market on exercise and fitness was booming. Why not incorporate diets into the umbrella of a fitness lifestyle?

16

Thus we had the dawn of the dieting era from the early 90's onward. Unrealistic expectations of slimness and idiotic standards of beauty began to be imposed on everyone, men and women. All of a sudden, if you weren't dieting, you were a loser.

We're far from those days now and to be honest, a lot of people do recognize the inherent lies in those ad campaigns. However, the issue is most of us have adopted newer lies to supplement those older ones. We still believe diets are necessary and that restricting our behavior, as if our bodies and minds are undisciplined little brats, is the only way to achieve health.

Health is, of course, this desirable physical image which approximates that of a model or an actor. Steroid use and diseases related to overdose has exploded since the '90s and this is a direct consequence of harmful imagery being presented as an ideal. All of a sudden, our bodies, which got along just fine from the days the human race were cavemen, could not be relied upon to decide what was good for them.

Our minds and brain, which dictate everything else in our lives, suddenly needed a re-education in what was good and for it. It's as if all of us woke up one day and decided "nope, thousands of years of evolution can't hold a candle to this new-fangled, science-y looking piece of advertising". The lies we tell ourselves have evolved these days.

Some people claim to not be on a diet but have weird notions about what, when and how to eat. Do not eat carbs after 6 P.M, do not eat fruits because they have too much sugar, do not eat bread, do not consume alcohol if you've eaten too much fat, do not look at the dessert menu because it's a full moon and you'll turn into a werewolf.

Alright, that last one might be an exaggeration. However, the point is any sort of food restriction is a diet of sorts. Food is not something to be restricted. This is something we'll look at later but the whole idea of some foods being better than others is flat out wrong.

All food is nutrition and contains calories that fuel us. Our bodies know, far better than that celebrity Instagram influencer, what to do with those calories. Restricting things just complicates our internal mechanisms and makes it that much more difficult to lead a healthy lifestyle.

Speaking of which, let's look at this lifestyle craze a bit more.

Eating not Lifestyle

People don't just eat food anymore. They are hardcore Paleo believers. Or Keto believers. Or Alkaline die-hards. When and how did food turn into something crappy to define yourself by? Did the world run out of fancy houses and Italian sports cars somewhere along the way?

Diets these days are not marketed as such. Instead, the word "lifestyle" has taken on an insidious character. Influencers on social media don't pitch diets anymore. They pitch a fitness "lifestyle". You see, it's not just what you eat, it's how you do everything! And presumably, that makes it all OK! No more diets BTW!

This is all a new fangled marketing ploy and once people catch on to this, the clever suits will invent another buzzword to get everyone hooked. It is important we recognize this for the outright lies that they are. A good rule of thumb when evaluating any such information is to see whether it demonizes certain food groups or activities (in the case of exercise and fitness).

Again, there is no such thing as good or bad food. There are no super foods or inferior foods. You don't need to watch your weight like a hawk and be obsessed over every single pound of fat or muscle you have. All kinds of restrictions are diets, even if they are not identified as such, and you need to steer clear of them. Let's take a look at why.

The Diet Cycle

We lightly touched upon, in the previous chapter, the weight fluctuation phenomenon that everyone experiences when adopting a diet and failing to live up to its unrealistic demands. Understanding the biological functions behind this phenomenon is crucial to understanding why diets, of any kind, are rubbish.

When we embark upon a diet, the first few weeks are generally stress-free. Our bodies are true marvels of evolution and adapting is what they do. Those first few weeks, which usually involve a restricted calorie intake (eating less than what you need) in order to lose weight, causes our body to adapt to lower energy levels and forces it to burn off the existing energy stores.

I'm going to get a bit academic on you here but bear with me. Our bodies use glycogen and fat as fuel. Glycogen is usually the preferred source and this is the first thing which is burned. When you begin to restrict calories, there's less glycogen coming in so the stores start getting depleted.

Glycogen has a side effect whereby, the more glycogen you store, the more water your body needs to store along with it. Thus, the less glycogen you have, the less water you need. Thus with the stores depleting during the first week of a calorie-restricted diet, your body decides that it's carrying too much water and sheds this weight.

This is why during the first week of any diet, people will almost always lose weight and think it's some sort of miracle. Actually, it's just your body getting rid of excess water due to reducing stores of glycogen. With your primary fuel source decreasing, your body then turns to fat stores to fuel itself.

Meanwhile, in the real world, you're eating less than you actually need to function as a person. Your mood gets affected because, quite literally, your brain has less fuel to carry out and process tasks that it's normally used to having. Your body has not fully adapted as yet and this manifests itself as being irritated or just not functioning at the levels you're normally used to. The net result is, even your dog begins to think of you as a sourpuss.

Right, now getting back to what's going on inside you. Your body begins to burn fat as fuel and given the stores available, there isn't much of a concern when it comes to finding it. You continue to receive energy from fat and during the second and third weeks, despite being a bit irritated, see some progress in the mirror. Perhaps some muscle definition and hitherto unknown muscles peeking out. Progress is great, isn't it!

However, this progress is merely occurring because of the fact that your body has not adapted yet. It still thinks you're in some sort of delusional phase and you'll eventually snap out of it and start providing it some glycogen again. As the days go by, your body eventually realizes you've officially lost it and begins to adapt to this new regime. This is good right? After all, a lot of diets advise on "giving your body the time to adapt".

Wrong again! What starts happening is your body realizes there's a food shortage and starts burning every single piece of food more efficiently to generate as much energy as possible. Since fat stores are getting depleted and since there doesn't seem to be any glycogen forthcoming, every calorie that cannot be efficiently burned is turned into fat for emergencies. Your body, in short, treats this prolonged calorie deficit as a massive worldwide food shortage.

Meanwhile, you think your diet is going well, despite the increasingly irritated mood you're in, and press forward. Soon, you realize you aren't making any progress anymore. Your body has adapted to the caloric deficit and is now doing everything it possibly can to keep you at the current state since it thinks anything below this will result in a free fall towards death. That's a tad dramatic but, hey, you can't argue with evolution!

Even worse, you realize you're actually getting fatter (because of the increased fat storage) and refer to your diet guide book for help. It says you need a caloric deficit to lose weight. So obviously, the solution is to increase the deficit by eating less. In turn, your body thinks the global food crisis has deepened and fights back even harder to keep you at status quo.

Your brain finally has enough, rebels, and everything becomes a point of irritation. Soon, your brain decides it's time to take over and directs your attention to food which you've been denying yourself. That sugar glazed honey donut which a few weeks ago was easy to ignore, looks like El Dorado now and eventually you succumb, since you have no choice. Your brain literally doesn't give you one.

And so, a few months later, you're right back to where you started. Except, you're not exactly where you started at. All that food crisis mania your body went through has taken a toll on it and it's now overcompensating by burning less energy than usual. It's over-cautious now since it keeps anticipating another crisis around the corner and wants to be prepared.

This is why your diets will always fail. They never had a chance of success to begin with, since they're directly opposed to who knows how many years of evolution. This is why your weight will fluctuate and eventually, you'll end up right where you began in terms of weight, but worse off in terms of health.

This is also why starvation doesn't work. If a caloric deficit was all it takes to lose weight then surely, it follows that completely restricting calories would lead to the highest amount of weight loss. Well, no since your body will just eventually give up and start burning muscle to sustain itself, once the fat runs out. Once you feed it again, it'll immediately convert everything to fat in order to stave off another possible starvation event which it anticipates to be around the corner.

Restricting Types of Food

Well, if restricting all food is bad and if the body can adapt, why not restrict certain types of food? Like say, consume only fat but not carbs (Ketogenic diet) or consume high carbs but no fat (HCLF/Atkins etc.)?

Our body is designed as a perfectly balanced mechanism. The various macronutrients present in food are required for many types of bodily functions. This is why the old adage of eating a balanced diet holds true.

Restriction of any sort, via fasting or juice cleanses or anything else you can think of, is a terrible idea and only makes it that much more difficult to be healthy.

Breaking Free

So if dieting is bad, what is good then? After all, for most of us, dieting of some kind has become the only way we relate to food and it can be quite a large leap to now accept that all food is good.

This neatly brings us to the first principle of intuitive eating, which is:

Rule#1: Unsubscribe from Diet Culture
This is easier said than done given the, previously mentioned, relationship most of us have with eating. Well, here's how you go about doing this:

PHASE 1- GET CLEAN

Accept the fact that all this dieting nonsense has clouded your vision and that you are in dire need of an intervention. You have been doing things the wrong way and enough is enough! Take back control over yourself by cleaning out all the diet books and other literature you have stored.

This applies to electronic stuff as well. Clear your browser history, hop on over to your social media accounts, and unfollow anyone who propagates these dieting and fitness lies. Mentally, remind yourself of how much harm your body undergoes when you diet. Re-read the previous section titled "The Diet Cycle" and burn this into your mind.

Clear out all those diet tracking apps and subscriptions you have NO exceptions!

PHASE 2- GET MAD!!

The best way to enforce a new habit is to get emotional about it. Your existing habits with regards to dieting are deeply ingrained and you will need a strong dose of emotion to uninstall those old beliefs and empower yourself.

Remind yourself of how everything is a marketing campaign and how people lie in order to make some extra money, even if it costs you your health. Look at the evidence that shows dieting doesn't work. Reject strongly any new-fangled diet that appears by reminding yourself it's all a new ploy to sell you something you don't need.

Take the time to appreciate how amazing your body is and how it's been protecting you all this while. You've misunderstood its intentions all along. What you thought was a lack of progress and frustration was actually a good thing. Your body was the only thing keeping you healthy, despite the damage you were causing. Truly appreciate how it knows what is best for you.

You may find yourself temporarily drawn to a new diet and begin thinking that this might just work. Get emotional about how you're being manipulated and reinforce your new found knowledge.

(Note: some of the statements about marketing and dieting might seem incendiary. However, it is necessary to get emotional about all this. Remember, you're being unreasonable in order to install correct beliefs about dieting. You're NOT embarking on some hateful crusade against mass media. This is about you, not someone else, and their actions have nothing to do with you.)

PHASE 3- RELAX

You're not perfect and neither is anything in this world. That's perfectly OK! You don't know everything and you don't need to. You have flaws and that's fine.

So go ahead and bask in your imperfection. You don't have to be perfect because you, as yourself, are perfectly more than enough. Feel the weight decreasing on your shoulders as you learn this. Treat yourself for educating yourself and for taking a huge step towards ensuring your health.

After all, you deserve it!

STEP 2- LOOKING FORWARD: DEVELOPING SELF KINDNESS

Now that you've broken free from the diet culture and its poisonous effects, it's time to take a long hard look at yourself. Don't worry, this doesn't mean looking at yourself with a critical eye but to actually learn how to evaluate yourself.

Most people complete the first step and think this is a license to develop bad habits but this is far from the case. In this chapter, you'll learn how to adjust your expectations to reality and to start aligning things in your life so as to get the results you deserve.

MINDFUL LIVING- EXAMINE NEGATIVE BELIEFS

Mindfulness is something you're probably familiar with. In short, mindfulness is the best technique to get you to live in the present moment and to be aware of what's going on around and within you. In short, being mindful gets you living in the real, present moment instead of worrying about the past or the future.

A wonderful side effect of mindfulness is the development of acceptance. You tend to realize that once you've given your best effort towards achieving a goal, it's pointless to worry about things you cannot control and your worry has zero effect on whether the goal is achieved or not. So you might as well relax and enjoy yourself!

Applying mindfulness to your body is crucial for you to overcome the negative beliefs you will likely have installed within you. You see, your beliefs will not just disappear overnight. As we saw in the previous chapter, before you make real progress, you need to work to remove these old beliefs that are responsible for holding you back!

We'll cover a mindfulness exercise later in this chapter which will help you relax and accept your body for what it is. First, though, let's look at some negative beliefs most of us have about our physical self-image. See which ones you have, and as you read along, really question them and ask yourself how much good have these beliefs done you.

Body Image Expectations

For most of us, an ideal or beautiful body image is a slim and incredibly muscular one. While there might be some difference in expectation between the sexes, this largely holds true. When staring at the mirror, all we evaluate are the areas which need improvement.

"My waist is too fat" and "My thighs are too big" soon devolves into "Why am I such a failure" and "Why am I so ugly". You don't need me to tell you that such thinking is harmful.

All of us need a serious talking to with regards to what the ideal body image is. We keep repeating these lies to ourselves and keep pushing ourselves to achieve this ideal image which might not even be right for us. Here's the truth: The ideal body image is that there isn't one!

That's right! There is no such thing as an ideal physique. "Ideal" standards are just something everyone made up. Back during ancient times, the ideal physique for a woman was considered to be something most of us today would consider plus-size! It's not just women either ("How Women's 'Perfect' Body Changed Through History")[1]. Do you know that historians have conjectured that all ancient Roman gladiators, to a man, had a gut ("What Gladiators Were Really Like | Cosmos")[2]? Even more surprising, the bigger the gut, the more successful and idolized they were!

If you're thinking this means the gladiators were fat, it's an indication of how your thinking has been warped. I said they had a gut, not that they were fat or obese. Those are two very different things.

These "ideal" labels are just made up and it's high time you recognize they ought to not have any power over you. The truth is that each one of us is different. Some of us are left-handed and some right-handed. Some of us have brown eyes and some green. How ridiculous does it sound when I say that blue-eyed people are inherently better than green eyed people?

Yet, while we accept this standard when it comes to eye color and have no issues with accepting diversity there, we have a major mental breakdown trying to accept the diversity of our bodies! It's perfectly OK to be different in everything else but all of our body proportions, for all 6 billion of us on the planet, have to be the exact same, within a few pounds of each other! Ridiculous!

This leads me to the next poisonous belief we have: Fat phobia.

Fat Phobia

To tell you the truth, this topic deserves its own book. No other belief has caused more harm than this one. Pursuing a so-called ideal, lean body image has led many people to despise the fat they carry.

It just so happens that one of the macronutrients which is essential for our bodies is fat. Putting one and two together, doesn't it follow that we should simply not eat fat? Shouldn't we all stop drinking cow's milk and drink goat's milk instead because the latter has less fat? Shouldn't we start consuming chemically processed marmalade in place of butter for breakfast?

Even more harmfully, this phobia of fat has been turned towards other people leading to horrible things like fat shaming and passing judgment on people just because they look fat. Ask yourself this: What is usually the first thing you notice about someone once you see them again after a long absence? "Wow, you've lost weight!" or "Hmm...she's put on weight". This is nothing but fat phobia in action.

Fat phobia also manifests itself as weight bias wherein people think there's an ideal weight everyone needs to hit in order to be healthy. Weight and health are two completely different things as we shall soon see.

Again, I need to stress here that I'm not claiming you ought to go around doing whatever you please and eat whatever you want, no matter how bad it is for you. What I'm saying is that you can work on improving yourself with an air of positivity. Just because you need to work on something doesn't mean you deserve to be ridiculed until you achieve the goal. For now, let's look at another metric of fat terrorism, the BMI.

The BMI Travesty

The body mass index was originally developed by scientists to measure trends in large samples of population data. In short, they needed something which could give a reasonable estimate, over a large sample size, so as to be able to monitor the overall health of the populace.

To take this bird's eye view type of number and to apply it to yourself personally is, frankly, one of the fitness industry's most ridiculous ideas. BMI is not a measure of your health. If it was, why is it that every highly functioning athlete has a BMI which classifies them as "obese"? Go ahead and let me know, I'll wait. The BMI is a useful approximation tool and when used correctly, it is extremely helpful. To use it as a gauge of your own health, however, is simply using it wrong. It's like using a hammer to install a screw. Of course, you'll fail!

Recent studies conducted on BMI data has actually shown that the group of people classified as obese are actually the ones who have the fewest instances of heart attacks, the disease most linked to weight gain.

Safe to say, BMI is not the metric you should be tracking or bothering with. Neither is your weight. All of this begs the question: what should you do instead?

DEVELOP TRUE KNOWLEDGE

Once you've completed the step of examining your beliefs, via mindfulness, it's now time to educate yourself on how things really are. We've already seen how everyone is different and has their own quirks. While it's easy for us to accept these quirks in people, somehow, we don't make the leap when it comes to body types and the image of health.

The reality is everyone is genetically different and it is this which defines our ideal body weight. In other words, your body already knows what it's ideal body weight (called the Set Point Weight) is and does not find it difficult to stay in that range. In fact, it will do everything it possibly can do to stay there. This is why, if your ideal body weight falls outside the mainstream "ideal" weight, your diets are bound to fail.

Our bodies have evolved over thousands of years and no amount of advertising and corporate imagery is going to change the way it functions. Most diets fail because they fail to acknowledge this very basic concept. This is why only a small minority of people succeed at dieting because their set point weight happens to fall in the range of the "ideal" body weight.

Thus, it's not the diet that's getting them results, it's their own body that's doing so! It makes sense that these people will be in a minority since how can the entire human population fit into such a narrow range?

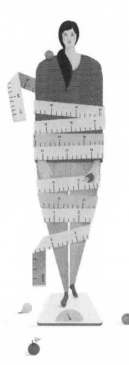

SET POINT WEIGHT

So is it possible to determine what your set point weight is? Well, yes and no. It is impossible to put a number on it in advance via any scientific method. It is possible, however, to feel your way to it. This is where mindfulness comes into play.

Our body is constantly communicating to us what it wants and what is good for it. It's just that we've become deaf to its signals. Why do you feel so bad or stressed when dieting? It's your body telling you that

32

this is not good for you. Your mental state is the best gauge of what your body wants.

If this isn't obvious as yet, the best way to get healthy is to work with your body and mind instead of against it. After all, one way has thousands of years of evolution backing it up. The other just has a skinny model on a billboard.

The first step to attuning yourself back to your body's signs and giving it what it needs to be healthy, is to practice self-acceptance and adopt a body neutral viewpoint.

Body Neutrality

As the name suggests, body neutrality is a mindset where you detach the idea of health from body weight. It is important for you to realize body weight is one of the many factors which determines health, not the be all and end all of health.

In a fantastic study conducted with over 11,000 people in the United States, scientists established the fact that it was possible to get healthier without any change in weight. People were subdivided into groups based on their habits such as consumption of vegetables and fruits, smoking, consumption of alcohol, and exercise regularity.

The study found that subjects who engaged in unhealthy behaviors such as smoking, drinking excessively, and not consuming fruits and vegetables, had roughly the same risk of disease, irrespective of their weight. People who cut even a single negative habit though, cut their risk of disease by half regardless of their weight.

This proves that your weight and the amount of fat you're carrying, unless you're an extreme case, has nothing to do with your overall health and your risk of contracting a disease.

Accept the fact that your body is smart and knows what's good for it. Start appreciating it and becoming more aware of what it's communicating to you.

Health Gain Not Weight Loss

It's high time we developed a more inclusive and practical approach to fitness and dieting. Instead of thinking in terms of weight loss or fat loss, we need to approach it as gaining health.

Seen in this perspective, fitness takes on an entirely new dimension, freed from the burdens of the tape measure or the weighing scale. We start acknowledging the diversity in body shapes and accepting flaws. Someone being fat or out of "shape" is no reason to shame them or hurl abuses at them, as some twisted form of "motivation."

Eating is viewed differently under this regime as well, since we're no longer eating or restricting food to maintain or attain a goal weight. Instead, we eat for the purposes of nutrition and to satisfy hunger (which is our body's way of telling us it needs food). Food is a way to nourishing ourselves, not a list of "allowed" and "not allowed" or good/bad etc.

Action Steps

The following exercises will help you develop your mindful state towards your body and will help you cast off those old, idiotic beliefs that have been impressed upon you. Practice these exercises regularly and you will reap the benefits of not just a healthy body but a healthy mind. Which is what "good health" means in the first place.

BODY ACCEPTANCE MINDFULNESS EXERCISE

Seat yourself in a chair, in a place you won't be disturbed for at least the next 15 minutes. Take a few deep breaths and notice how your body tenses up when you inhale and how all of it dissipates when you exhale. Gently close your eyes and acknowledge how your body feels.

You could be experiencing some sensation in a part of your body. Your hands might be cold for instance. Take a moment to admire how wonderful your body is! Observe how your heart keeps beating of its own accord, providing you with life at every instant. Note how strong and capable your legs are, and how they always support you.

Notice how your stomach feels and take care examining the sensations you're currently experiencing. Examine your chest, back and neck, all the way to the top of your head. Notice all the sensations you feel throughout your body and just stay in that moment. When any thoughts distract you, simply smile internally, and direct your focus back to your body, wherever you desire.

Practice this for 15 minutes every day and you'll become more in tune to the rhythms of your body and mind.

Fat Phobia Awareness

It isn't enough for you to intellectually know that fat phobia is a condition that you have learned over the years. You need to examine it and remove all traces of it. Correcting behavior has three steps:

1. Acknowledge the problem

2. Awareness of manifestation

3. Reinforcing correct behavior

Step one is taking the time to realize how poisonous fat phobia is and how it negatively affects you. Notice how it constantly makes you the judge and jury and how contrary to nature it actually is. It literally sets you up to judge the way this world has been created since you're rejecting the diversity inherent in it. Rewind the clock in your mind and see the various ways in which this has harmed you or caused you to harm someone else.

Step two is becoming aware of the ways this belief manifests in your day to day life. Do you find yourself judging people because of their weight? Do you beat yourself up when you visit stores because you can't find clothes in your size? Are your fitness goals in line with health or weight? Are you exercising to become healthy or to attain some billboard advertising ideal?

Step three is consciously reinforcing correct beliefs and actions. Catch yourself in the process of judgment and tell yourself why this is incorrect. Apart from positioning yourself as an unkind person, realize how you're simultaneously judging yourself as well. Remind yourself that the fact that the store doesn't have clothes your size is their problem, not yours. Remind yourself that the goal of exercise is to get healthy, not look like a model.

Developing Appreciation

Write down a list of ten things you're happy about when it comes to your qualities. You're a kind, loving person who loves his/her family and so on.

The key to this exercise is to do it as fast as possible. Don't worry about the number 10, it's not a list-making exercise. Simply list out all the things you love about yourself. Do this exercise every morning when you wake up, before doing anything else.

Take the time to really think about all the amazing things and skills you have. The key is to develop an attitude of gratefulness, which is actually in line with how our natural state is.

Notice and Acknowledge. Then Move On

We are constantly bombarded with images of what we ought to look like and how we need to be living our lives. It is almost impossible to keep up with the various lies we're being fed via advertising.

One solution to avoid all of this is to retreat into nature and become a hermit. Now, as wonderful as that sounds, it really isn't a practical course of action for most of us. Therefore, we need to deploy our awareness when it comes to a situation where we're being fed the usual "diet" information.

The source of the information could be anything. A media piece, a friend, a co-worker, your boss, whoever. The exercise requires you to acknowledge, mentally, that what you're being told is a lie. Remind yourself of the information you've learned thus far in this book and recall what sort of negativity these sort of statements spiral into.

Next, mentally decide that you reject this sort of rubbish and will not allow this negativity to pollute your being. Don't express this to the source of all this since there's no point trying to convince anyone else. Besides, their beliefs are their own. You may express your beliefs to them but avoid getting into an argument over "right" or "wrong".

Simply recognize how misguided they are and move on with your life. It is not your business to change their world view. Your job is to live with happiness and acceptance of the wonderful creation that you are. So relax and stretch yourself into this acceptance!

STEP 3- HUNGER: WHAT THEY DIDN'T TELL YOU

We've seen thus far how it's important to simply sit back and let your body dictate to you what it needs. Your body communicates these needs by sending certain signals. Hunger is one of the biggest signals there is and is a perfectly natural biological process.

Hunger has, however, been twisted into something else and thanks to constant dieting most of us have a weird relationship with it. This chapter will clear the air over hunger and teach you the normal, natural way to relate to it.

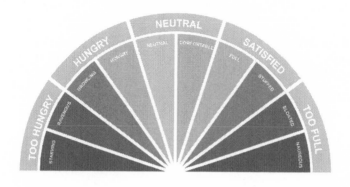

THE HUNGER SCALE

HUNGER AND GUILT

Hunger is a sign that we need to feed ourselves. Even children know this instinctively before they can even speak. As adults though, we've done some damage to this pretty straightforward mechanism by imposing rules onto it, such as caloric deficits and the like.

A lot of diets call for calorie restrictions when trying to lose weight and as a result, we've grown accustomed to ignoring or trying to wish away our hunger pangs via willpower or external methods like smoking, consuming caffeine, or drinking water. After reading the previous chapter, I hope the irony of doing this isn't lost on you.

As a result, we've taught ourselves that hunger is a bad thing and ought to be ignored. Hunger also makes us feel guilty since if we're restricting ourselves, our body signaling for more food is a betrayal of our diet regime. How can we improve ourselves when our own bodies are against us?

Eventually, nature wins out and we satisfy our hunger by binge eating and losing all semblance of self-control. In other words, we live between extremes. This see-sawing between hunger and emotional extremes is what causes weight fluctuation, as we saw in a previous chapter, and is why diets will never work.

Here are some issues you will probably face thanks to restricting your hunger in this manner.

Lack of Awareness of Hunger

It stands to reason that if you keep suppressing your hunger, eventually, your brain becomes numb to the gentler sensations of hunger. Only when it reaches a full-blown, manic state, does your brain wake you up and you begin to associate hunger with an extreme feeling of needing food.

The reality is hunger operates on a scale. You are supposed to feed yourself when your hunger pangs are gentle, and avoid the extreme hunger that strikes when you constantly deny the requests of your body.

The key to health is to just listen to your body. Unfortunately, you might have dulled this connection quite a bit. There's no reason to worry though. Using the exercises listed later in this chapter, you will learn to re-establish this connection.

Guilt

This one's a major problem for most dieters because it puts you squarely in a position from which it becomes easy to mistrust your body and to think of it as a traitor of sorts. You put in all that effort to stick to a diet and all your body does is go and get hungry.

You try to devise solutions to trick it into feeling full, like chewing some gum or drinking water or smoking. While this dulls the hunger it never really goes away and this leads to even more frustration.

Eventually you capitulate, giving into the now unbearable hunger and binge eating. This is breaking your discipline and is counterproductive to your goals so you end up feeling guilty. Even worse you imprint the image of yourself as someone who is undisciplined and cannot be trusted to achieve something onto your self-image.

All because you started off with a misunderstanding over the nature of hunger and your body.

Bad Eating Habits

All ignoring your hunger does, is mess around with your eating habits. Suddenly, your regular meals become inadequate to fill you and you begin binge eating; cheat meals become a source of pleasure, even though they cause a hefty dose of guilt afterward.

This cycle is almost impossible to break out of via the usual dieting regime. Even worse, your brain begins to associate pleasurable eating with guilt and this is how eating disorders start. This is why some people develop disorders whereby they feel the need to puke out what they just ate.

Here's the thing: If you notice that your most enjoyable meals are the ones where you're cheating on your diet, then it's time to quit the diet and learn once more what hunger really is, and fix your relationship with it.

THE BIOLOGICAL PROCESS

This section is going to get all scientific on you so fair warning. It is still necessary for you to understand all this in order to drill into yourself that hunger is a perfectly normal and natural thing to experience. It's not something to feel harassed about.

Hunger is caused by a combination of hormones. It is these hormones which provide a signal to your brain and cause you to feel hungry. Regular signs of hunger are a perfectly normal biological process and are nothing to get alarmed over. In fact, regular hunger pangs are an indication of good health since your body is well tuned to your needs and your metabolism is high.

Having said that, the exact process by which our hunger signaling system works is not fully known because a large majority of it involves neurotransmitters within our brain. Given our limited knowledge of our brain, all we can successfully observe is the biological process which occurs when our food stores run low.

Hormones and Neurotransmitters

Our hunger mechanism is dictated by a combination of both hormones and neurotransmitters. Hormones are secreted by the endocrine system within our bodies and neurotransmitters are produced by neurons within our brain.

Hormonal effects tend to last longer and have greater effects on organs further away from where they are secreted. For example, insulin is a hormone. It is produced in the pancreas and travels great lengths to help metabolize food which is ingested.

Neurotransmitters, by contrast, are localized and act a lot faster than hormones. Sometimes, their effect can be almost instantaneous. A good example of this is Serotonin which impacts our gut health by effectively dictating the quantity of food that passes through it.

Ghrelin

Ghrelin is also known as the hunger hormone. It is usually secreted in the stomach and within the intestines. Its secretion depends on the lack of or abundance of food within us. The mechanism by which it operates is fairly straightforward.

The larger the amount of food deprivation your body undergoes, the larger the amount of Ghrelin that is secreted. Once the hormone enters your bloodstream, your brain, specifically the hypothalamus, receives the signal and translates this as "I'm hungry".

This could be accompanied by gentle rumblings in your stomach and a feeling of an empty stomach. The more you ignore this signal, the larger the amount of Ghrelin becomes, until you can't ignore it anymore. Your body's reasoning is simple and uncomplicated. If you're hungry, you need to eat.

The concept of restricting your diet or eating less than you need doesn't really come into the equation and is simply deemed unnecessary.

Neuropeptide Y

Also called NPY, this is a neurotransmitter which is a hunger stimulant. NPY is produced along with Ghrelin and while Ghrelin is a general hunger signal, NPY is a carb specific signal.

Why carbs specifically, you might be wondering? Well, remember how we saw previously that carbs, specifically glycogen, is the primary fuel source for our bodies? Stands to reason then that our body has a special transmitter which reminds us to fuel up. NPY is produced in conjunction with Ghrelin and functions in much the same way when you ignore it. Its signals simply increase over time, the longer you ignore it, and eventually, you are left with no choice but to give in. This is why, when hungry, a loaf of bread or something covered in sugar looks particularly tempting. It's your body pushing you to refuel yourself, for your own good.

Biologically Engineered

As you can see now, our bodies are literally engineered to not work on a diet or any form of calorie restriction. The minute you restrict calories, your body generates signals which only get louder until you cannot ignore them. Once these signals get loud enough, this usually results in us eating something to quickly reduce them and this is where a lot of damage is done.
The priority at this point, when the signals are too loud to ignore, is to quickly eat something, anything at hand. Hence, gorging yourself on snacks and fast food becomes the norm and while your body receives its fuel, you're not really eating healthy food. Thus, the cause of you eating unhealthy is actually your diet!

SETTING THINGS RIGHT

Given all this information, hopefully now you can understand that hunger is a perfectly natural process and isn't something that should or can be controlled by willpower or some such nonsense. Giving into hunger is normal and is what you should be doing.

The damage is caused when you ignore hunger and it builds to unreasonable levels. This is when you cannot help losing self-control and overeating unhealthy food. The reason for this is not the hunger or your lack of willpower, as your diet guide will claim, but the fact that you ignored your own biological processes in the first place!

This is why diets fail and most dieters regain the weight they've lost within a few months of losing it. They're constantly hungry and thanks to ignoring the warning signs of hunger, not only do they damage their ability to listen to the warning signs, but they also attune their bodies to dial up the hunger signals to an extreme since they don't respond to the more subtle or gentle signs.

Repairing this relationship is essential to intuitive eating and it's high time you take back control of this. Restrict your food no more and see how much healthier you will be!

Get Rid of Diet Mentality

This is something you ought to have done in step 1 but it's a good reminder nonetheless. Get rid of all your diet trackers, calorie counting charts, and any other tools you might be using to track your eating habits.

Unplugging from all of this will force you to rely only on yourself to figure out when and how much you should eat. This is the normal order of things and it's important you carry out this exercise all the time.

EXPLORE HUNGER

Write down how you feel prior to, during and after your meals. Remember, your meals are now dictated by how you feel! When you become aware of the hunger pangs, take a moment to get to know this feeling.

If you've been dieting for a while, at first, your hunger signals will seem highly amplified. This doesn't mean your body is incapable of producing signals of a lesser intensity, it's just that you're not tuned into the lower amplitude signals as yet. This is fine and you will eventually adjust and become more in tune with your hunger rhythms.

Practicing mindfulness at this stage is essential. You need to explore how your body feels in the moment, how your mood feels, and be on the lookout for any sensations. This does not mean you need to sit and meditate when you feel hungry! Go find some food, eat as healthy as possible, and all the while keep scanning yourself. Mindfulness does not mean a lack of activity!

It is important to also monitor how you feel mentally and physically as you eat. Knowing yourself when hungry is half the equation. You also need to get to know yourself when full. As you eat, your hunger levels decrease and you will feel fuller. Get to know this progression from "empty" to "full" and stop eating when you feel full.

Again, if you're used to your portion sizes being dictated by something external, all this will feel weird at first and you will not trust yourself. You need to understand that making a few mistakes along the way is perfectly fine and normal. Your body isn't some fragile thing that will break if you happen to eat an extra 100 calories.

Trust yourself to figure this out and know that your body is designed to survive with health. It knows what it needs and knows how to make you get it. So let go of the need to control, sit back, and enjoy the ride!

Break up Your Meals Equally

Some people are used to dividing their meals disproportionately throughout the day. Some choose, for example, to have a heavy breakfast and heavy lunch followed by a light dinner with no snacks in between.

This has a harmful effect since it changes your relationship with your hunger signals. When breaking meals up this way, the only hunger pangs you will be conscious of is when you're extremely hungry, since you're full most of the time, and as a result, will not be able to see the difference between binge eating and plain old eating.

If you've been doing this, make sure your meals are all roughly the same size and have a couple of snacks in between, whenever you feel the need. By evenly distributing your meals throughout the day, your body won't experience a sudden drop in nutrition and won't need to dial things up in order to get your attention.

Meal Times

Remember that nothing external should dictate when you eat your meals and this includes the clock. Eat only when you feel hungry. If you feel hungry after just having eaten, eat some more, instead of feeling guilty about it.

Hunger is not something to get guilty over and as mentioned before practice mindfulness at all times to know your patterns better.

A Lack of Trust

I understand that adopting all of this immediately is a big ask. After all, you've been conditioned to think of eating and dieting a certain way all your life and now, suddenly, someone pops up and tells you to do things you've not done for a long time.

Building trust with your body and its mechanisms is crucial. After all, if it were possible to summarize the intuitive eating principle in one sentence, it would be, just listen to your body. It sounds simple but is difficult to practice.

There are a number of objections that arise as a result of your prior conditioning. Let's take a look at some of them and see if we can clear the air a bit.

Can I Eat Only When I'm Hungry?

Eating when you're hungry is what's best for you. Responding to early signs of hunger reduces your risk of type 2 diabetes and other diseases. This point should be obvious; it's good to listen to your body but it tends to get drowned out with all the hysteria over diets.

An important point to make here is that intuitive eating is not a diet regime. Eat only when hungry is not a hard and fast rule you need to absolutely follow. If you anticipate a situation in the next few hours, for example, where you won't be able to eat and you will probably feel hungry, it's perfectly fine to eat something in advance to carry you through that period. Remember, the key point is to stop worrying about food and just feel your way through.

Won't I just Eat All the Time? What About Discipline?

This question arises from the diet mentality which conditions you to stop believing in yourself. Under any diet regime, our bodies and minds are the enemies which are forever trying to take us off track and destroy our health. Somehow, this ridiculous point is so well marketed that it seems to make perfect sense.

Scientific research has shown that people who eat when hungry and generally respond to hunger cues manage to self-regulate their food intake a lot better. In addition, eating in this manner reduces insulin sensitivity and enables better control of blood sugar levels.

In short, stop worrying so much about your food. Understand that all these objections are a result of the lies you've been fed (in place of adequate food) over the years and you need to just let go and listen to your body and mind.

But I'm Never Hungry!

This is a side effect of extreme dieting as well. Thanks to constant yo-yoing of your body weight and health, eventually your metabolism drops to lower levels and you just don't eat as much anymore.

Even worse, some people develop alternate ways to crush their hunger, which they feel guilty about, by smoking or drinking something in place of food. This is a tough place to be in but at the beginning, eat 3-4 meals per day with some snacks and give your body some time to recover.

If you've been following this pattern for a while, perhaps you've developed an urge to smoke every time you feel hungry. Monitor yourself for these signs and eat something instead. Mindfulness around your meals and hunger is the key to recovery.

I'm sure by now you can see what a difference this approach is from traditional dieting methods. Isn't is a whole lot easier and doesn't it feel, just, free?

Just a quick side note: if you feel like you want to share your journey with me, discuss what you're struggling with or how you're making progress, join our **Facebook group.** Permitted Fruit – Intuitive Eating. Here we want to bring together a community of like minded people who can support each other.

If you feel like sharing your thoughts on this book, I kindly ask you to leave a review on Amazon or Audible. It would help me spread the word and help more people, thank you!

STEP 4- EATING: WHAT THEY DIDN'T TELL YOU

If our relationship with hunger is fraught, it's nothing compared to how we view food! All the guilt, frustration, and lack of trust we place on hunger is equally, and indeed in greater amounts, transferred to food.

Food has gone from being a source of nutrition or fuel to becoming this unsolvable puzzle of superfoods, garbage foods, high-fat foods, eat this and not that, and so on.

It's time to take and step back and repair this relationship.

MINDSET AND FOOD

How many times has something like this happened to you? When on a low carb diet, you begin to crave bread. When on a high carb diet, you begin to crave cheese. If you can't eat grapefruits, why is it that you immediately begin to think about them? Do me a favor right now and quickly do NOT think about an Elephant.

How many of you thought immediately of an Elephant? We may not fully know how our brains work but we do know this very well: The worst possible way of weaning ourselves off anything is to demonize or deprive us of it. This thing which until recently was a perfectly normal object suddenly becomes the shiniest object in the world and we absolutely must have it.

We see this happen all the time when it comes to teens and alcohol and tobacco. Earlier campaigns that focused on stopping teenage smoking only served to increase the prevalence of teenage smokers. Anyone who has set foot on a college campus on a weekend (or even leading up to a weekend) knows the glamour with which alcohol is treated by those experiencing a lack of parental supervision for the first time in their lives.

Dieting has a similar effect on us. By denying us something, we unwittingly glamorize it and all of a sudden, bread or cheese or whatever, becomes like treasure.

Deprivation and Scarcity

While the exact mechanics of this sort of behavior is not known, we can take a good guess at why it does happen. The natural order of our minds is one of abundance. In other words, our minds do not perceive a lack of anything naturally. Anything which we think of as limited is learned from our environments and from those around us drilling it into our heads.

This is sometimes good for us, as in the case of a baby trying to stick its fingers into an electrical socket, but sometimes it can be quite harmful to us, as in the example of inheriting a prejudice against someone. It seems as if our minds cannot process the state of "lack" logically and goes haywire when something is restricted. This is why, the object of lack or the thing we try to ignore and cut out of our lives, ends up becoming the very thing we obsess over.

When it comes to dieting, this deprivation mindset plays out exactly as you would imagine. The moment your diet tells you to stay away from a particular food group, you pretty much doom your chances of success since you've set it up as something special and forbidden. This forbidden fruit becomes hard to resist and it takes a lot of strength, mental and physical, to direct your focus away from it.

Eventually, as we've previously seen, your defense mechanisms breakdown and you can't resist anymore and you simply give in. Instead of simply eating the forbidden food though, people begin engaging in a new pattern born from this deprivation mindset.

The Deprivation Backlash

Here's a simple picture for you to imagine: Let's say you've been on a diet which forbids you from eating chocolate and red wine. Suddenly, you begin to see red wine and chocolate everywhere you go. You're strong though and by using "willpower", whatever that means, you resist the temptation.

You know your diet regime has only been prescribed to you for 6 weeks. That doesn't seem so long! Sure, the 4th week onward, you really begin to struggle but by reminding yourself that it's just 2 weeks to go, 1 week to go, 3 days to go, you pull yourself ahead and make it to the end. Your nutritionist now prescribes you another diet where all bread is forbidden.

What about chocolate and red wine though? Oh, that's perfectly fine, she says. Great! What's the first thing you do? Go buy some chocolate and red wine of course! You might even throw an end of diet party and celebrate with your friends, telling them to bring over some red wine and chocolate! By the end of the night (or early morning), you've gorged yourself on wine and chocolate and don't want to ever look at another piece of chocolate or grape again.

This story doesn't sound too outlandish, does it? The process of celebrating the release from a diet is often termed the deprivation backlash and it leads to a number of harmful eating habits such as rebound eating, which is what was described in the example. As you can imagine, gorging yourself on something that is forbidden makes you feel like a pig or a glutton, and it imprints the image of someone who is undisciplined and cannot be trusted onto your self-image.

All because you decided you could not have a piece of chocolate and sip some wine! Let's look at some of the other habits that are a product of the deprivation mindset. Check to see which ones you've indulged in previously or are even currently experiencing. Doing this exercise will make you a lot more aware of what's going on around you and is the first step to healing your relationship with food and eating.

Last Supper Eating

This phenomenon occurs right before adopting a new diet. You know a restriction is coming and compensate beforehand. Think of someone who decides to quit smoking from tomorrow and starts binge smoking today. The net result is, if this person used to smoke half a pack daily, they've now smoked two packs in a day, all with the justification of "it's my last day".

This sort of behavior only reinforces the mindset that what we're about to attempt is impossible, and that it is beyond our strength to accomplish. Naturally, we fail at the task and feel guilty. Adopting new, restrictive diets plays out the same way.

We fear the deprivation that's about to occur and try to compensate for it beforehand. As we go through the diet and experience deprivation, our natural mechanisms kick in and we eventually succumb and break the rules of the diet. The net result is, yet another failed diet and yet another instance which marks us out to be undisciplined.

All of this only lowers our self-esteem and if we happen to be someone who society deems "fat" or "overweight", you can only imagine the dark places this leads to.

Grab it While it Lasts

This pattern of eating is a form of rebound eating wherein a person views food as something scarce. This is a common occurrence with someone who grew up in a large household where food was either scarce or there was a lot of competition for it. Even if the food was not actually scarce, eating in a large group often causes us to eat faster because of the fear that there might not be enough left over for us.

People who indulge in this pattern tend to carry this over to all venues of food and whether they eat alone or with someone else, they tend to grab everything at once, eat as fast they can inhale, and end up with a bloated and upset stomach thanks to improperly chewing their food.

This sort of eating paints food and meals as something joyless and as something to get done with as quickly as possible. It's an inconvenience and a burden. You can imagine how much pressure such a person would then put themselves under once they being a diet. If something is so unimportant, surely it must be easy to control. When the diet fails, suddenly this person, in their mind, has failed at something that should be easy to achieve.

Special Occasion Eating

Despite the name, this pattern isn't confined to eating habits around special occasions or festivals. The special occasion could really be anything our mind deems as special. For example, it's not uncommon to see college students returning home for the first time gorging themselves on home cooking.

Another example is when visiting a restaurant that is, perhaps, out of someone's regular budget. The temptation is to eat as much as possible as quickly as possible and ironically, this leads to a complete lack of enjoyment when it comes to the food. Suddenly this special restaurant was not really worth saving up for.

Eating something you receive as a gift is a great example of this. A bag of cookies gets demolished before anyone else has the chance or can even look at them. Perhaps you receive as a gift some food you've heard a lot about and have always wanted to try. Next thing you know, you've gone through the entire box or packet of them and can't bear the thought of eating more of it.

All of these patterns beg the question: If dieting is actually against our natural order how is it that some people succeed at it? How do some people push through all of this and achieve their goals? Well, these people simply fall into another eating pattern born from the deprivation mindset called restrained eating.

Restrained Eating

People who make diets work for them learn to substitute their mental patterns for some external signal. So instead of letting their bodies control them, they set up external rules that dictate how they should eat and what they should eat. Such people are usually chronic dieters and by externalizing the justification, they manage to stay on track.

For example, if they feel hungry and it isn't time to eat as yet, they justify the lack of food by telling themselves it isn't time to eat as yet. By blaming the clock and by convincing themselves the clock is what determines meal times, they manage to pull themselves through their diet. Such actions are often mistaken for willpower and are admired within traditional dieting circles as if it's something to be emulated.

What is actually going on is that these people are setting themselves up for a fall much harder than the normal person since the body's mechanisms cannot be ignored forever. As the discipline required to stick to the diet becomes more and more extreme, eventually even the tiniest of gaffes causes such people to classify it as "overeating" or "breaking the rules".

When this happens, it's as if the floodgates on a dam opens and all that pent up frustration and deprivation floods in and they cannot control themselves. This is why you'll often see healthy looking people immediately put back on a ton of weight the minute they give up dieting. It's just the pent up release of all the deprivation they've subjected themselves to.

All of these patterns spring from a very definite psychological state. While the manifestation of the individual patterns differ, all of them follow a basic psychological pattern as we shall see next.

PROHIBITION VERSUS SHAME

Dieting and all diets put us in a very peculiar situation. You see, they all force us to play a game of tug of war between prohibition and shame. This is something we're not even aware of when we begin. I mean, after all, we're trying to get healthy right? Where do shame and prohibition come into it?

It is important for you to understand this psychological state of being because more than anything else, it is this that explains why diets fail, why you cannot lose weight on a diet, why your weight seesaws up and down, why your mindset gets so poisoned on a diet etc. In short, this is the thread that connects everything. So buckle up and pay attention!

When we begin a diet, on the surface of it we're telling ourselves what is and isn't allowed to be eaten under the garb of getting healthy. In doing so we set up the prohibition of certain foods as an important step to success and simultaneously we also associate guilt or punishment with the consumption of these foods.

So for example, if your diet does not allow chocolate, you immediately enter a deprivation mindset with regards to it. Now, you justify this mindset by telling yourself that prohibiting chocolate from your diet is good for you.

Any attendant bad feelings that arise are pacified with this thought process. Meanwhile, you're also telling yourself that if you were to succumb and eat chocolate, you'd be breaking a major rule and making yourself unhealthy. In other words, if you eat chocolate, you'd be "guilty" of doing so.

At the beginning the sense of duty towards prohibition is high. After all, you've just begun. As the days and weeks go by though, that chocolate starts looking mighty tempting. You pull yourself together and tell yourself to be disciplined. In short, your sense of prohibition helps you stick to your diet and be "disciplined".

This sense of prohibition is kept alive by your willpower. Your sense of shame is also low since, after all, you're not consuming any chocolate. There's a limit to your willpower though, which like any muscle gets tired when deployed without rest, and eventually, you give in and have a nibble of that delicious chocolate.

Immediately, your sense of prohibition has reduced. Simultaneously, your sense of shame has increased, thanks to you breaking your rule. Now, for your sense of prohibition to be high, your shame has to be low. As we saw in the previous paragraph, your prohibition is supported by high willpower and low levels of shame. Your willpower has long since disappeared thanks to relentless use. Shame has also increased since you've had a little chocolate.

The net result is your sense of prohibition has nothing to champion its cause and as it reduces, you begin to take larger and larger bites of chocolate. Your shame keeps increasing with every bite you take and this, in turn, reinforces the lack of prohibition. Think of it as a vicious circle. The more you eat, the greater the shame and the lesser the sense of prohibition.

Eventually, your willpower returns from its vacation, fully rested and ready to get back to work. Much like an office executive returning after vacation only to find the building on fire, it rushes in with a sense of alarm and gets right back to work, pushing the sense of prohibition back up. This manifests as you suddenly "snapping out of it" and realizing what you've been doing.

Chocolate, thus, gets banished and you get angry with yourself for having broken your rules. This anger, which is really your willpower exerting itself again, banishes the shame back down to new lows and your sense of prohibition is at an all-time high. Eventually, though, your willpower beings to get drained again due to a lack of rest and disappears without notice, presumably dreading what it knows is about to happen.

This leads us right back to the breaking of rules, the increase of shame, and the decrease of prohibition. Your willpower once again returns in disgust and props you up. All while this is playing out in your subconscious mind, you alternate between feelings of duty, guilt, and rage. Is it any wonder you lose focus and everyone around you notices you're moody all the time?

This sort of battle can never be won due to the fact that both the feelings of prohibition and shame are set up in a tug of war between each other. People who diet often think this is correct for some reason and instead blame their willpower for letting them down. This is quite tragic since it's the willpower which has been ensuring what little discipline there is, given the impossible situation it has to work with.

Diet guidebooks also preach the same philosophy and mention the need to stay strong and focused. That's a bit like someone telling you to focus on finding a quarter in a cluster of bushes while there's a hurricane blowing about you. Your lack of focus or strength is not the real culprit here.

So what's the solution? Well, much like you would be daft to go around looking for loose change in the middle of a storm, you are behaving in an equally idiotic manner by accepting this tug of war between prohibition and shame as valid. You see the key to succeeding at anything is to simply relax and let it come to you.

All of this is a fancy way of saying, sit back and get out of your own way. Let your body and mind guide you. Instead of trying to win the shame versus prohibition game, refuse to even participate. The minute you do this, I guarantee, you'll see the sun shining through once again and it is this peaceful state of mind which brings you results.

Not some fanciful calorie restriction nonsense.

Your 4 Step Healing Solution

I'm not going to beat around the bush anymore. Here's the 4 step process which will heal your relationship with food and put you back on the right path with regards to getting healthy. They are:

1. Educate Yourself

2. Evaluate Yourself

3. Indulge Yourself

4. Monitor Yourself

Let's look at each of these steps in greater detail.

Educate Yourself

This first step is akin to a cleanse. Not the juice or detox cleanses you've been urged to try out, but a real one. It's time to learn the realities of food and to understand that all forms of food are nutrition and fuel. That's it.
There's no such thing as a good food or a bad food. That slab of butter is just as good or bad for you as is that pile of sweet potatoes and pumpkin seeds. The key to health is moderation in everything and finding the sweet spot is not your concern.
This might seem counter-intuitive but the reason it's none of your concern is because your body will let you know. Just like there are biological processes to let you know when to eat, there are equally powerful processes that let you know when to stop. Your only job is to maintain balance in everything.

Another key piece of knowledge you need to drill into yourself is that there is no such thing as the perfect diet. Those perfect diets which are being marketed as such are far from it and, as mentioned previously, determining what is ideal is easy. Simply take a look at whether the diet calls for a restriction of anything. Yes? Toss it!

The categorization of food runs a lot deeper than just good or bad. There's naughty food, guilty food, guilt-free food, everyday food, special food, sometimes food, the sun rose from the west food and so on. Alright, one of those is made up. However, each one of those labels is as ridiculous as the other. Food is food. It's meant to fuel you. It's not special or a medicine or anything else.

The food you eat is a part of your overall health and is not the only determining factor. Thinking otherwise is simply playing into the diet mentality.

Evaluate Yourself

What descriptors are you using for food? Do you find yourself gravitating towards a particular label for food? For example, do you find yourself favoring low carb options or low-fat options? Do you find yourself purchasing "guilt-free" options?

What are your beliefs around eating like? Do you automatically feel guilty eating some types of food like chocolate or cake etc.? Do you feel like a pig and beat yourself up if you eat something that you enjoy too much? Sounds ridiculous when it's written that way but it's what you've been practicing while on your diet.

This exercise will help you come to terms with what's going on inside your head when it comes to food. Take a piece of paper and headline it with the label "Food is..." and then begin to write down everything that comes into your mind. Do not restrict yourself in any manner and simply let the words flow out.

Compare what you've written with the knowledge you received in the previous step and indeed, throughout this book thus far, and see where you're on the wrong track. Do not be alarmed or upset if you find major differences and don't beat yourself up if you feel sad for following incorrect advice this long.

Instead, follow what was recommended in Step 1 in the second chapter of this book. Reread it again, realize why you think the way you do, and keep telling yourself you're on the right path now.

Indulge Yourself

Simply thinking and being mindful isn't enough. You have to actually "do". On a piece of paper, write down a list of foods you have been told are bad for you and that you ought to avoid them like the plague. Also include things you've wanted to try but have been depriving yourself of, thanks to a diet.

A caveat before we proceed: Foods that are highly chemically processed like TV dinners and foods which have ingredients which are full of chemicals (for example lamb shanks which don't need refrigeration and can last for months on end) are obviously to be avoided. We'll be covering what to eat in a later chapter but for now, just keep this in mind.

Now go over your list and pick out one or two items. Ideally, include one item you would like to indulge in and one which you've always wanted to try but have felt guilty doing so. It's now time to conduct research! Buy the first item and stock it in your home. Make sure it's always available to eat and go ahead and eat it. If you feel any guilt, go back and remind yourself of everything you've learned thus far. Listen to your body as you eat. Monitor how you feel, how empty your stomach is, how full you feel etc.

The idea is to get used to listening to your body when eating. Stop when you feel full. With the second food item, try it out in a restaurant or somewhere else and if you like it, feel free to stock it in your home. Carry out the same mindfulness procedure described in the previous paragraph; monitor how you feel and really listen to yourself.

Monitor Yourself

Carry out the previous three steps over and over, you'll soon find your relationship with food healing. Suddenly, you'll find food is normal and that no food is better than the other. There are some things you like and some you don't. This is perfectly normal.

The underlying attitude you need to have at all times is to monitor yourself. Always keep checking in and evaluating how you feel. At first, you won't know what's going on but keep at it, and you'll soon learn to distinguish between the feeling you get when you eat something tasty and when you eat something you don't like.

I'm not talking about just the taste but also how it feels within, how your brain reacts to it, and so on. By listening to yourself constantly and by being on the lookout for signals, you'll find your body communicates everything it needs to you, crystal clear, and you don't need to be afraid of food anymore.

Speaking for being afraid, these 4 steps are a lot more radical than they appear at first. After all, I've just asked you to toss out the rule book you've been following and instead of giving you a new one, I've simply said listen to yourself. This will naturally be intimidating and a number of conflicting thoughts will be popping up in your head.

Well, let's take a look at some of these and see whether we can address them. Largely all fears will follow some variation of the list below:

- I'll gorge all the time without restraint

- I don't know what's healthy so I'll eat unhealthy food always

- I've eaten what I want before and it didn't work

- I simply don't trust myself

- Without strict rules, I won't have any discipline

It's perfectly normal to have fears like these come up. It is your duty to take these in stride and act anyway. After all, this is what courage is and it takes courage to change. A major aid to courage is to understand things as they truly are. Think about it. What is it that we fear the most? The unknown.

Right now, you don't know how you'll react or what's going to happen when you adopt these new behaviors. It is so different from what you're used to hearing. Well, instead of tackling these fears one by one, learning about a psychological principle called the habituation response will help you understand why they crop up in the first place and to also eliminate them from existence.

THE HABITUATION RESPONSE

As we've previously seen, the deprivation mindset has the inadvertent effect of glamorizing the very thing we wish to banish. The habituation response is the opposite of this. While things that are banished occupy a special pedestal, things that are ordinary simply don't seem as shiny as they once were.

It's easy to look at examples of this in real life, outside of food. That car you were saving up for and spent years trying to afford stopped being as desirable once you actually started living with it day to day didn't it? Most of the clothes you wear once must have looked or made you feel like a million bucks but these days, you simply throw them on and lounge about your home.

This is the habituation response in action. The good news is it applies to food as well. Psychologically speaking, habituation is simply a decreased response to something upon repeated exposure. Once you stop viewing a certain type of food as something special, it loses its sheen and you will naturally moderate your intake. This is why step 3 of the healing process, indulge yourself, calls for stocking the previously forbidden food around your house.

Yes, initially you will feel the rush of freedom and eat more than you should. However, given that there's nothing restricting you anymore, you'll begin to reason that you're acting irrationally and your brain will immediately begin to dissociate this food from pleasure. Your relationship to it will be back to normal.

In a study conducted by scientists, a group of women were fed macaroni and cheese every day, every meal, for a week. While the women were extremely enthusiastic at the beginning, by week's end let's say their enthusiasm was a bit dimmed. The entire point of the healing process is to readjust your food thermostat to normal levels.

You've been operating at extreme temperatures for so long, you've lost touch with what food actually is.
The process of intuitive eating builds up your ability to trust yourself once more. You see, you're not some mindless machine which screws everything up unless it is told exactly what to do. All of us have a wonderful, inbuilt guide within us and all we need to do to stay healthy is to listen to that voice.
Intuitive eating is as much a process of staying healthy via mindfulness as it is a healing process for your body and mind.

STEP 5- BANISH THE FOOD JUDGE

All those old beliefs and impressions formed in your mind are not going to clear themselves out overnight. It takes time, awareness, and patience to get rid of them. Some of these inner voices are harder to let go of than others.

So let's take a closer look at them and see their true nature.

FOOD FUNDAMENTALISM

All of us are guided by an inner voice which is really just the sum of all our beliefs and thoughts about any particular topic. Now our thoughts usually lie somewhere on the spectrum between enlightened or ignorant or fundamentalist. The more our thought tilt towards the enlightened side of things, the better our lives generally are.

Fundamentalist thought is characterized by some very recognizable signs. Generally, fundamentalist beliefs are born out of a narrow view on things and tend to be quite harsh. When our beliefs about food tend to take on fundamentalist characteristics, it can be quite difficult to get rid of them, since such thoughts tend to be the loudest.

A key point to always remember is that this type of thought process is not rational and is reserved solely for those who have a perverse wish to feel miserable. Taking back power from them requires you to always remind yourself that you deserve to be happy and anything that makes you miserable does not deserve a place in your mind.

A Lack of Grey

The food judge which resides within us does not understand subtlety. Something is either the worst thing in the world or it is the equivalent of heaven. Sugar is a surefire way for contracting stage 4 cancer or is the sweetest of all sweet nectar and there's nothing wrong in eating 1,000 spoonfuls of it daily.

The truth is that life, in general, is full of gray. Much like how every situation has two sides to it, every food has a good and bad side to it. This is perfectly normal and is how things should be. Another insidious way this judge pipes up is by getting us to punish ourselves for eating a certain kind of food.

A good example of this is to forego dinner if we overeat during snack time by even a little. It causes us to feel bad about ourselves and only pushes us further into a hole. This voice may sometimes also sound extremely knowledgeable and say things like "carbs are full of sugar and excess sugar gets converted to fat" or "fats are the biggest reason for the distertation of our bloodstream. An excess of it activates the nodal probes and increases the risk of heart disease".

That second statement is completely made up by the way. A lot like how that statement sounds smart but means nothing, the food judge is also constantly making up stuff it thinks is correct. Sometimes knowledgeable, sometimes pessimistic, sometimes confusingly optimistic, sometimes rebellious, the food judge has plenty of tricks up its sleeve.

Despite the tone of voice, an easy way to spot it is to check whether the belief being expressed has any semblance of moderation to it. If it's all black and white, you know what it is you're dealing with and where it belongs.

The Negativity Bias

Why is our inner voice so fatalistic though? Why can't it just chill out and just take a break from constantly being on edge with things? A big reason for this is simply the way we're engineered as human beings.

Back when our ancestors were crawling around in forests, eating whatever they could find while simultaneously avoiding become something else's dinner, this ability of our brain to prime them to look for danger in everything enabled them to survive. This is why human beings are capable of surviving in extremely hostile conditions and in those situations, this negativity bias is a great tool to have.

However, on a bright sunny day, in the middle of a park, facing a picnic basket hamper, the negativity bias doesn't really have much to do. It can't just switch off though since we don't have the ability to do that (as yet). Therefore, it pokes holes in your sandwich or finds unheard of dangers in that perfectly innocent blade of grass.

In many ways, it's not your brain's fault that it talks this way. It's funny to think about but, the very existence of the negativity bias proves that everything has a good and bad side. This bias protects us in dangerous situations but harms us in safe ones. Food, and indeed everything else in life, behaves in much the same manner. Everything has a safe limit beyond which it just becomes bad.

The world exists in gray, not black and white. Realizing this and the existence of your negativity bias is the key to making informed decisions when it comes to food and silencing the food judge. Anytime you hear the voice pipe up, ask yourself: is there any particular reason I should feel threatened right now? Does my food judge have a degree in nutritional science to be able to determine what is good or bad? Rationality always tends to get rid of poor thinking and this is no different.

Understanding negative emotions and experiences also goes a long way towards reducing your negativity bias. Given its inherent bias towards the negative, our brain always gives greater weight to incidents and emotions that feel worse. In other words, bad emotions feel much worse than good emotions feel good. We experience sadness much easier and to a higher degree than we do happiness and joy.

Therefore, it is critical to understand that when you feel bad or you feel as if you'll never make progress, this is just your brain amplifying things way out of proportion. We'll discuss combating negative thinking shortly but for now, remember that you are engineered to absorb negative experiences fast and better than positive ones.

Therefore, it takes a lot of positive reinforcement to get rid of a little negativity. This is why repetition and constantly reminding yourself of what you've learned thus far is critical, even though it might seem excessive. Overcoming a natural bias is not an easy task after all.

All or Nothing Thinking

This pattern of thought is a cousin to the "lack of gray" type of thinking pattern and has similar "Alice in Wonderland" characteristics. In this type of pattern you'll end up believing that life is a series of direct consequences to your actions.

While this may be true in a larger sense, the day to day pattern hardly works like this. An example of this thinking is "I need to eat perfectly every single day or else I'll become fat". While it is true that you need to eat healthy in order to remain healthy, notice how this perfectly sensible statement is twisted by the words "perfectly", "fat", and "every single day".

Suddenly we're looking at something which has an entirely different meaning and this colors our perceptions accordingly.

Glass Half Empty Syndrome

It's a well-known fact that optimists tend to live happier lives than their pessimist cousins. If anything ought to signal that everything in the world has two equally true sides to it, it should be this fact. Yet, many people confine themselves to the pessimistic side of things under the garb of being realistic or practical, whatever that means.

This pessimistic thinking often leads to a negative spiral where bad things become worse. Statements such as "I'm not losing weight" turn into "I'll never lose weight, I'm hopeless". Needless to say, this is hardly a healthy mode of thought.

NEGATIVITY BEGONE!

Right, enough with all the doom and gloom. You're here to learn how to banish this inner food judge of yours and it's time you learned how. Now that you're aware of the patterns of thought that creep up, the first step is to simply observe and become more aware of them occurring.

Do not judge or admonish yourself for having these thoughts. You cannot be a ray of sunshine every single moment. It's perfectly fine to feel sadness and feel down sometimes. This is life after all remember? The thing that's full of grays?

The next step is to examine and snap out of incorrect expectations of what success looks like.

Not a Straight Line

Most people assume success is a straight line angled upwards at 45 degrees when viewed left to right. The reality is a lot more confusing. Success is filled with false starts, retreats, failure, and restarts. It's a squiggly line and is a lot more unclean than what you might think.

Exploring the true nature of success is beyond the scope of this book but I highly recommend you read the book *Psycho Cybernetics* by Dr. Maxwell Maltz. Dr. Maltz breaks down how our brains are engineered for success and scientifically explains how failure is a necessary part of success. The trick lies in viewing failure as feedback, not as a result.

The book explains it far better than I ever can so I highly recommend you check that out. Meanwhile just remember the mantra: Failure is feedback, not a result.

Change Your Language

This is especially helpful if you're a glass half empty kinda person. The next time you get into your usual negative spiral, examine your language. Perhaps you're stuck in traffic on the way to work. "Man this is the worst!". Using a phrase like "the worst" is a pretty extreme way of expressing something.

Once you become aware of using extreme negative language, immediately correct yourself. "No, this traffic isn't the *worst,* it's annoying me a bit". Expectations are again the key here. Pessimistic people tend to think in absolutes and when deploying this technique, they tend to expect an instant jump from negativity to bliss.

It doesn't work that way. Your focus should simply be to improve your mood a little bit. Reduce the negativity by a small degree and simultaneously increase the positivity by a notch. Chocolate is not "bad for your health". It "tastes great and is fulfilling in the right quantities". Sugar is not "processed shit", it's "something that makes my life sweeter".

DO NO HARM

I'll admit, I'm plagiarizing this one from The Buddha. One of the founding principles of Buddhist philosophy is to "Do no harm". A lot of people make the mistake of thinking this means you ought to watch your step all the time in case you step on some unfortunate ant.

This completely misses the point that "Do no harm" extends to ourselves. We are our worst critics and while we're perfectly kind to others, we judge ourselves harshly. If you indulge in all or nothing type thinking or pessimistic thinking, this is your medicine.

Track your thoughts as you become aware of them and when you notice any extreme, fundamentalist statement you utter about yourself, such as "Why am I so fat? I'm such a loser" or "Stop eating that donut piggy", pull yourself up, get mad, and tell yourself that this sort of talk is completely unacceptable. It is not OK to talk to yourself this way.

How would you react if a complete stranger insulted one of your loved ones in this manner? You wouldn't sit there and continue what you were doing, would you? So why would you accept it when your food judge talks to you this way?

Love yourself first and always.

STEP 6- LEARN TO LISTEN: FEELING FULL

We've already looked at the process of hunger and how important it is to listen to your hunger cues. As part of that chapter, we had looked at some fears that crop up as a part of the process of listening to and trusting yourself.

The signs of fullness are the most important ones you need to heed to in order to allay those fears. The process of knowing when you're full is no different from the usual mindfulness techniques we've been covering throughout this book as you will see.

Connecting with your mind and trusting it to tell you when you're full is a process and one you should nurture.

THE SCIENCE OF FULLNESS

Much like hunger, in fact exactly like hunger, feeling full is a biological function. Much like the fuel indicator light in your car, your stomach is capable of telling you when it's empty as well as when it's full. We fully trust our fuel indicator lights but somehow think our stomachs are untrustworthy when it comes to knowing what it wants.

Biologically, the entire process is controlled via hormones and receptors in our brain. Our stomachs are receptacles for food which process it and slowly release it into the small intestines. Once the stomach is empty, our hunger mechanism kicks in, and eventually we start eating food.

The food we eat begins to fill our stomach and as this happens, it begins to grow in size. There are a number of intricate nerves around the stomach whose job it is to detect changes in size. As the stomach gets bigger, these nerves signal the brain that the stomach is becoming full physically.

Nature, being what it is, didn't leave us without a plan B for letting our brains know when our stomach is full. Perhaps anticipating that some diet regimes will call for filling that stomach with water in order to trick it into feeling full, our bodies have multiple backups to detect whether its real food or some placebo being ingested.

The small intestine has a number of pH detectors which measure those levels in your bloodstream once you begin to eat. The more you eat, the greater the by-products of the digestive process, like fatty acids and enzymes, and all of these change the pH of your blood.

Once these changes are detected, our body concludes that it's real food that's being ingested, not water or coffee, and our endocrine glands release hormones within our system which notify the brain that the hunger signals are being heeded and that it's perhaps a good idea to reduce their intensity.

This results in a reduced feeling of satisfaction as we continue to eat. The hormone most responsible for signaling the brain that we're getting fuller is Leptin. As more Leptin is produced, the stomach relaxes more and more thereby delaying the passing of food into the small intestine. This fills up our stomach and via Leptin, our brains know we're full and this is the time to stop eating.

This full feeling is both physical and emotional. You usually will feel satisfied and just not feel like eating anymore. Also, your stomach will expand as well leading to the "full" feeling. Leptin is the key to all of this. Unsurprisingly, dieting and reduced calorie intakes result in decreased Leptin production.

The exact biological reason as to why this happens is not relevant. Suffice to say, if you stop using something for the purpose it was intended for, your body will simply stop producing it at its original levels since there doesn't seem to be any use for it. When you restrict your food, you barely ever produce Leptin since you're constantly hungry. Think of it as your body falling out of practice with producing Leptin.

The side effect of this is once you diet for a long period of time, it becomes difficult to pinpoint when you become full. You need to practice getting that feeling back and use it to guide you once again.

The following techniques will help you regain touch with that full feeling once again.

REGAINING THE LOST TOUCH

Before we get into the techniques it bears to keep in mind that there is no single parameter which applies to everyone when it comes to feeling full. Everyone has their own levels and the last thing you should do is to judge yourself based on how much everyone else is eating.

One person may be able to consume an entire plate of food whereas you may feel full after a few bites. This is perfectly OK and there's nothing wrong with you. Part of getting back in touch with yourself is to break out of the need to have rigid rules to eat and to simply trust your body to figure it out and let you know.

The other thing to mention is that you will make mistakes. If you're not used to listening to yourself at all then it stands to reason you're not going to be very tuned into what's going on. You will end up under eating and have to eat soon after a meal. You will end up overeating as well. This is perfectly fine and your body is not going to explode just because you screw up a few times.

So, with a calm, relaxed mind, and without expectations of any miracles or special insights, let's look at how you can get back in touch with yourself.

Don't hurry

Cook and eat in a good mood

Feel the taste of food

Soft, relax music

Drink more water

Mindful eating

Eat your favorite food last

Respect your body and health

Sit at a real table

Not multitasking

Meal Timing

You're probably used to timing your meals as per the clock. Well, it's time to ditch that. It will be difficult to get a feel for how full you are so the best thing to do is to notice how long it takes after a meal for you to get hungry. This has an additional effect of ingraining into your mind that it's normal to eat and then get hungry again after a few hours.

Once you've eaten a meal and stopped eating when you reasonably approximated that you were full, keep checking in with yourself every 20 minutes or so to see how you feel. Notice the physical sensations and also your mental levels. Are you alert and able to focus on the tasks at hand or do you feel foggy?

Is your stomach growling with hunger soon after you ate? No matter, eat once again! It's perfectly fine to do this and if you've been following a diet plan all this while, this sort of thing is going to happen a lot at the beginning.

Scanning

Conducting periodic scans of your body and mind is essential to discovering your fullness signals. There's no correct time to conduct a scan simply because there's no such thing as a correct time.

Make your mind up, when your day begins, to constantly check in with yourself and to scan your hunger or fullness. As you're eating your meals, get to know what it feels like to have your hunger constantly decrease to the point where you aren't hungry anymore and are full.

This might be a bit difficult to comprehend at first but there's a difference between a lack of hunger and feeling full. You see, hunger is something that can always return so if you only eat to the point where you don't feel hungry anymore, you'll notice that you always need to eat shortly after your meals. Feeling full is a step beyond the absence of hunger and is accompanied by a different set of feelings or a state of being. This differs for every person so it's not possible to describe how this will feel for you exactly. The key is to keep scanning always.

Scanning yourself during the middle of your meal is also a good idea. You don't need to drop everything and start meditating! Just take a few seconds to scan yourself and monitor how you feel. This ability to listen to yourself is a muscle and it gets stronger with regular exercise.

Don't worry if you're unable to figure anything out the first few times. If you've been dieting for a while then it's natural to forget this connection. Keep at it and keep practicing, you'll soon see results.

Judging Overeating

You will eat past the point of fullness quite a bit when starting out so don't worry about it. The real challenge here is to treat this as a normal occurrence as opposed to the end of the world. Unfortunately, dieting culture has demonized any overeating as being undisciplined and worthy of shame.

Snap out of this and realize that you will make mistakes and that it is by making mistakes you gain feedback as to what's correct. Therefore, making mistakes is a good thing. So if you do realize that you've eaten too much, take a step back, and forgive yourself. Remember what you learned in the previous chapter: Do no harm!

It also pays to document what it is you thought you overate. You see, sometimes we can't help but let our unrealistic expectations creep up on us and simply noting it down, forgiving yourself, and moving on is the best thing to do. With a calm mind, when you're relaxed, take a look at what you thought the additional portion was. I'd warrant it's usually a perfectly reasonable item like a scoop of ice cream or extra sprinkles over dessert.

Reclaim Satisfaction

Food is supposed to satisfy us. It's supposed to make us feel happy. Without food, not only would we all die out but lose an invaluable way with which to express ourselves. I know I've been hammering on about how food is food and nothing special but the truth is, a lot of us define ourselves by the cuisines we like and the food we eat.

Now that you've seen how harmful diet culture is and unplugged yourself from it, there's no harm in admitting to enjoying your food. Gaining satisfaction from your meals has an added advantage. By remaining satisfied and eliminating hunger, you'll simply eat less later on, thereby bidding goodbye to those cheat meals and midnight snacks.

What do You Like to Eat?

Prior to your meals, ask yourself, what is it that you love to eat? Are you thinking about eating some specific thing today? Have you been wondering about it for a while now? Well, go ahead and eat it!

This takes you out of the prohibition and shame circle we looked at earlier and obliterates the deprivation mindset. By eating the things you want to eat, when you feel hungry, you'll increase your appreciation of food and heal the poisoned relationship you've had thus far.

Explore Your Food

Take the time to get to know the thing you're eating. There are a bunch of sensory factors that go into any food. How are the flavor profiles distributed within this thing you're eating? Do you even know what the flavor profiles are? In short, they are:

- Sweet

- Sour

- Bitter

- Salty

- Umami

Uma what? Go ahead and look into it! Get to know what kind of food will give you this flavor profile. How can you enhance some of the profiles you like?

Eat Correctly

Given the painful relationship most people have with food, they tend to eat improperly which leads to poor digestion later on. Take the time to chew your food and really taste it. Nurture your palette and develop it by tasting new things.

Taking your time to chew your food also has an important biological function because this act triggers the secretion of enzymes in your body which helps digest your food better. In addition, the more you chew your food, the lesser the air you ingest and the lesser your chance of feeling bloated or gassy after a meal.

Hence the saying, "don't chew with your mouth open."

Know When to Eat

The key to enjoying your food is to eat at the right time. When you're feeling ravenous, you will, naturally, end up swallowing your food instead of chewing it. Now, it's not a big deal if this happens a few times but constantly doing this will simply damage your relationship with your food as well as your hunger signs.

Learn to discern between raging hunger and the first mild symptoms. Make your mind up to eat when the signs first start instead of waiting for it to bloom into a full-blooded crisis.

Using the techniques listed in the chapter on hunger will help immensely here.

Pay Attention

You are not a multitasker. There, I said it. A lot of emphasis is placed in workplaces these days on how we all need to multitask as if this is something praiseworthy. The reality is our brain cannot consciously focus on two tasks at once.

Therefore when you eat, focus on eating. It will be difficult since most of us are used to watching the television or playing with our phones when we eat. Focusing on food when eating will help you build appreciation for it and help you with all the previous tasks above.

STEP 7- FEEDING YOUR FEELINGS

Food is emotional, there's no getting around it. Right since you were a baby, crying for attention when you were hungry, there's always been some emotion attached to consuming food. This is perfectly healthy and reasonable.

What is not reasonable, however, is using food solely as an emotional coping mechanism. A lot of us literally eat our feelings and don't even know about it. What is the safe way to navigate this and how can you tell if you have an issue?

Eating is Emotional

Food has always been associated with emotion in every culture around the world. Food is used to signify, romance, family, happiness, sadness and so on. There's absolutely no harm in associating food with these feelings, even if they are negative. There's a lot of material out there which warns about emotional eating and that sort of thing but it really isn't as big of a deal as some of the other addictions that exist out there.

All of us are emotional eaters to a large extent. The key is identifying when food becomes a way to suppress our emotions instead of a way to express them. All food that is eaten tends to fall on a scale of emotions which broadly fall into the categories below:

1. Gratification

2. Comfort

3. Avoidance

4. Numbing

5. Guilt

These levels, as you can see, go all the way from positive emotions to deeply negative ones. Let's take a closer look at each of them.

Gratification

As we saw at the end of the previous chapter, eating to satisfy your taste buds is a perfectly natural thing to do. Exploring the taste of something you've often wondered about is how normal engagement with food occurs. In this emotional state, you appreciate eating and don't associate food with guilt of any sort.

What's more, eating in this manner actually keeps you in touch with yourself and you will avoid overeating and stuffing yourself.

Comfort

All of us associate food with family. How many of times have you fondly remembered your mother's cooking? How many times have you seen something advertised as "just like mom made it." Eating food for comfort is perfectly fine as it allows you to lower your stress levels and simply enjoy food for what it is.

If you're not feeling well and need some TLC, food often plays a huge role in that. Take note though, this level of emotion only associates with food in a healthy manner. In other words, you recognize food for what it is and don't feel the need to constantly fill up on your go-to comfort snacks.

That would be moving into emotionally negative territory which begins with the next level on our scale.

Avoidance

If you've had a shitty day at work and just need to curl up in front of the TV with a warm blanket and a few spoonfuls of Nutella, you're eating in a healthy manner. However, if you turn to the Nutella every time you get stressed or every time you have a rough day, there's something wrong that you need to fix.

Emotional stress is a sign from your body that things are not right and that you need to take some action to fix things. Eating in this state actually distracts you from those warning signals and is unhealthy.

Aside from letting your problems stack up, unresolved, you also end up overeating since by not staying in touch with your emotions, you're also severing the connection you have with your body's signals of fullness and hunger. In short, you're re-enacting the prohibition versus shame tug of war via another source.

Numbing

Eating in this emotional state is comparable to turning to alcohol or drugs to sedate yourself from the real world. People often turn to food in such states due to a feeling of being out of control and not being able to figure out what to do. Naturally, this only intensifies the feeling of hopelessness.

It is important to recognize your behavior pattern if you are, indeed, using food to anesthetize yourself from life. This sort of behavior ought to be nipped in the bud. While the physical damage it causes can be limited in the short run, it can always bloom into a pattern which can be extremely difficult to get rid of, much like any addiction.

Guilt

Guilt works on us in many ways. Self-hatred and feelings of inadequacy often express themselves as guilt, a feeling of "I'm ashamed of myself, I'm just not good enough". When thinking this way, a lot of people will force themselves to eat something they know is bad for them as a way of punishing themselves.

This pattern of eating is just another way to confirm what people already think about themselves. It takes an extremely negative mindset and instead of improving it, simply sets fire to it and destroys any semblance of hope.

Disconnecting from all or nothing type of thinking and practicing kindness (remember "do no harm") is the way out of this mess. If you are in this habit pattern, you owe it to yourself to treat yourself better. The problem isn't with food or even you. It's just with your thought patterns.

These eating patterns don't exist in a vacuum. All of them are triggered by certain events. More accurately, they're triggered by your reaction to certain events. Let's take a look at the triggers of unhealthy eating.

TRIGGER #1- BOREDOM AND EXCITEMENT

The biggest reason people eat when they aren't hungry is because they're either bored or they associate food with a reward. In the former case, it's the classic example of you lying around the house, not knowing what to do so you nibble on a few crackers or chips.

In the latter case, you may have planned an outing to a favorite restaurant or you may finally be allowing yourself to eat that previously forbidden food. This is a classic example of the deprivation mindset and highlights the importance of practicing food neutrality.

TRIGGER #2- FRUSTRATION, STRESS, AND DEPRESSION

These negative mental states provide ripe moments to overeat and eat when you're not hungry. If you're experiencing frustration, eating food gives you the dual advantage of doing something you can control as well as taking your mind off the thing that is frustrating you. Stress eating works much the same way.

In the case of depression, it's merely reaching out for something, anything that can make you feel better. Food, being associated emotionally with happy moments and connection (family, friends etc.), is a substitute for those feelings which seem to be missing.

TRIGGER #3- REWARD

From a young age, we've associated food with reward to varying extents. Behave well and you get ice cream. Clean your room and you can have dessert. While this tactic is perfectly fine in small doses, the issues arise when it becomes a habitual pattern.

This behavior crosses into adulthood as well when this is the case. "I'll finish my work and then have dinner" or "I'll run 5 miles and then allow myself a snack". The crazy thing is this type of thinking is often presented as being disciplined.

95

Speaking of discipline, food offers a reward in the form of a release to those folks who have an unbearable amount of discipline in their lives. If your life is perfectly, suffocatingly, structured to the point where every single minute is scheduled and planned, then food often provides a release.

The point I'm trying to make is that you need to be as disciplined as you can handle. If you take it beyond your limits, which is unhealthy, you'll find yourself looking at food as a release valve.

Reduce and Eliminate Emotional Eating

Emotional eating can be banished via mindfulness. You've already learned some of the techniques previously. You can use them to detect when you're emotionally vulnerable and to interrupt your usual pattern on reaching for food when this is the case. Some of the other techniques you can use are listed in the following sections.

Detecting Vulnerable Mindsets

Checking in with yourself and practicing mindfulness is the key to eating healthy, as you were meant to. A good idea is to journal your thoughts throughout your day. It's difficult to constantly keep checking in so, journaling, say every hour, is a good way to stay in touch with how you're feeling and your thoughts.

It doesn't have to be an elaborate essay. Just a few sentences like "I'm feeling happy right now" or "I'm frustrated with xx" and so on. Acknowledge the feeling, accept it, focus on your breath and move on.

If you find that the feeling still persists, conduct a full body scan in a place where you won't be disturbed for at least 5 minutes. Take this time to examine how you're feeling and tell yourself it's OK.

Develop Alternatives

You're using food as a distraction when you eat to cope with your emotions. Begin to develop alternative methods of reducing your food dependency. Examples include talking to someone you trust and are close to, reading a book, punching a cushion or pillow etc. Do whatever it takes to distract yourself.

Distracting patterns could even be something as simple as simply zoning or forcing yourself to smile. No seriously, when you feel bad, physically force yourself to smile an evil joker laugh. The physical act of smiling conveys to your brain that something is off and things can't possibly be as bad as it thinks it is.

Physical Patterns

Are you sleeping enough? Are you exercising enough? Are you eating balanced meals and allowing yourself to eat what you like?

Lack of sleep and exercise are amongst the primary reasons for developing an emotional imbalance. When you haven't rested well enough, your mind simply cannot cope with the regular stresses of the day and resorts to emotional crises.

This is why stress, anxiety etc. are triggers for emotional eating. Make sure you get a good rest and apply the concept of intuitive eating to sleeping as well. Go to bed when you feel sleepy and wake up without the aid of an alarm clock.

This is how we were designed to sleep and if it takes 10 hours, so be it. Sleep is often an equally fraught area like food. Banish the thought of being lazy or of needing "just" 4 hours of sleep as if you're Superman.

How Kind Are You?

This is a mindfulness technique and you can use this to keep a check on how kind you're being to yourself. Are you respecting yourself and your needs? Are you indulging in things that make you happy? Are you restricting something out of guilt?

When you journal at the usual time every hour, include a sentence reminding yourself to be kind to not just everyone around you but to yourself. Scan whether you were unkind or harsh to yourself over the preceding hour and instead of admonishing yourself, simply accept the mistake, tell yourself it's perfectly fine to make mistakes, and move on.

How Has Food Helped You?

If you're an emotional eater, it's easy to view food in a negative light. To repair this and as a way to enhance your food neutrality, ask yourself, how has food helped you?

Has it fueled you to where you are today? What are your happy experiences with food? Has it helped you connect with someone?

Make a list of the positive attributes of food and keep reviewing them periodically.

STEP 8- WHAT IS YOUR BODY ASKING?

Exercise. If diet culture has an evil twin, it has to be exercise culture. Get shredded, get lean, become functionally fit, adopt the new PcXv90 workout program and blast the fat away, and so on and so forth. Poisonous exercise culture deserves its own book to be honest. (Actually, now that I think about it...). For now, a chapter is more than enough to snap you out of this bad mindset and look at exercise and movement, in particular, intuitively.

The Truth About Exercise

Exercise is one of the best stress busters there is. We all know this. The reality is that it doesn't take a lot of exercise to become fit. What is tough is living up to that Instagram influencer's idea of what fit is. Washboard abs and muscles popping out all over the place is not the only way of being fit.

Much like how there's no single diet that works, there's no single way of becoming or being fit. Your body knows what it needs and how much movement it can withstand. Ultimately, your body and mind want to feel good. Exercise and movement is a way of doing this, so get out of your own way and simply listen.

Thought Shift

Fitness has suffered from the same ills that diets and food have. Much like how we've been told that diets equal health, we've been bombarded with the message that looking perfect equals health. "Perfect" of course is yet another set of standards that are imposed upon us, as if every human being on the planet is supposed to look exactly the same.

The all or nothing thought pattern often gets applied to fitness as well. Instead of simply moving, you need to "push till you feel the burn". Instead of running or cycling, you need to feel a runner's high. Instead of practicing Yoga, you need to do "power yoga", whatever that means, while stripped down to your underwear.

How often have you felt guilty about the fact that you haven't thrown up after your workout? This might seem ridiculous to ask but a lot of fitness programs actually treat this as a normal occurrence. If you aren't close to passing out, I mean, do you even workout bro?

A lot of guilt gets created as well with this type of thinking. Suddenly, food is positioned as the enemy which makes you fat. Your fitness routine is the only thing between you and a life of fatassery (yeah, that's a word bro, look it up) and food is something which is earned in sweat and puke.

It's time to snap out of this ridiculous thinking by reminding ourselves that our bodies know best what they need, not some gym freak hopped up on bro-science. Exercise is supposed to make you healthy. Not thin or not burn calories. Those might be the side effects but the real reason is better health. Here are just a few things exercise is good for:

- Reduced risk of:

  - Dementia

  - Breast Cancer

  - Depression

  - Heart attacks

  - Diabetes (Type 2)

- Reduced mortality risk

- Healthier blood pressure

- Increased lean muscle mass

- Increased strength

- Better cardiovascular performance

- Healthier cholesterol levels

You might be thinking that you already know all this and have tried exercising but it never seems to work out for you. Much like diet plans, exercise plans seem to fail for you as well.

THE EXERCISE PLAN FALLACY

A lot of people combine exercise with a diet plan and this is simply asking for trouble. The diet plan, in and of itself, is an unscientific thing and combining it with an illogical exercise pattern makes things worse. A lot of diets will call for limiting calories.

Well, the thing about limiting calories is that it places stress on your body. If you push that already stressed body even further in the gym, it should come as no surprise that eventually, your body and mind are simply going to scream "no more" and you avoid the gym along with binge eating.

This has an added negative effect of associating exercise with punishment when really, exercise is supposed to be good for you. People who have trouble sticking with exercise of any sort usually tend to load up on it at the beginning and end up doing too much too soon without giving their bodies time to adjust.

Thus, exercise becomes associated with failure and if you follow this path, it becomes difficult to motivate yourself to get up and exercise once more. After all, why would anyone voluntarily punish themselves?

Motion and Movement

The key to reconnecting with exercise is to begin with being kind to yourself. Exercise is not supposed to cause you stress or to make you feel guilty. Much like eating, exercise is an intuitively guided activity and your body and mind will let you know when it's time to go move.

Focus

Too much exercise is focused on the program itself, instead of on your own body. Look at any program and all you see are sets, reps, weight numbers, exercise form, and the number of minutes you're supposed to move.

This is true even for exercise programs which masquerade as general fitness tips. A popular one is to walk 10,000 steps every day. While the intention this program springs from is a good one, it completely turns the original intention of exercise on its head.

10,000 is not some magical number for you to aim at and neither is the amount of times you're supposed to lift a weight. Start focusing on how you feel when you exercise. You see, it's not necessary to follow a particular plan of action at the gym. Do what feels good to you and invigorates you.

Exercise is supposed to leave you feeling refreshed and energetic. A lot of people have trouble accepting this and tend to use adjectives like "punishing" or "hardcore" when describing workouts. From now on, simply focus on how your body feels when you exercise.

Monitoring yourself is not restricted to just exercise times of course. You will already be monitoring yourself throughout the day, so make a note of how you feel when you're inactive. Contrast that to how you feel after or during exercise. Odds are, you'll feel better overall even if the particular exercise movement makes you feel uncomfortable.

Remember, it's not about feeling good all the time. It's about feeling good most of the time and on a larger scale. The idea isn't to monitor and ensure you're feeling good from one minute to the next. That would be impossible. Instead, compare how you feel over blocks of time, separated by activities. How did you feel before breakfast? After breakfast? Before lunch? After lunch? During your siesta? During your workout? And so on.

Intuitive eating and exercising is not a program for you to rigidly follow and do not fall into the trap of punishing yourself over it. If you feel the need to begin a particular exercise program, great, go for it! All I'm saying is, monitor yourself physically and avoid working out to a particular numerical standard, such as X number of reps or X amount of time spent running on the treadmill.

Perform the activity called for as needed. If you find yourself unable to push as long as you program calls for, stop, and take rest. There's no need to beat yourself up or push yourself till you're close to passing out.

Exercise for Health

Your number one reason to exercise should be to get healthy, not to lose weight. It's time you consign the idea that exercise and weight loss are one and the same thing to the trash can.

Connecting your weight with exercise is a surefire way to get discouraged since the weighing scale becomes your reference point for success. Your body weight will fluctuate naturally within the set point weight limits and this is perfectly normal. If you've had a poor workout and you see that the scale indicates a couple of extra pounds gained, you're more likely to think your program is bad, you're failing etc.

Remove this type of thinking from your head and get back in touch with what exercise really is for. As long as you feel progressively better, you're on the right track.

Watch Out for Common Traps

One of the common traps that you will have to avoid when it comes to exercise is thinking that your workout is valid only if it satisfies a certain number of conditions. If you don't run for an hour, you didn't really run at all. If you don't work out in a gym, it's not really exercise.

This latter one is an especially harmful one, because remember, exercise is about movement. Not just lifting weight or running on a treadmill. Do children lift weight at the gym? No, they don't. Would you ever think of children as being inactive? Of course not. In fact, a child's inactivity is often a sign of something being wrong.

Climbing the stairs, walking in the park, playing around with the monkey bars, all of these are perfectly legit ways of getting your exercise in. Always remember to focus on how the movement feels to you. Get comfortable monitoring your body's movements. Sometimes, if you've moved too much your body will communicate that it needs to rest. So go ahead and listen to it instead of pushing yourself to go to the gym.

Another trap to avoid is to mistake activity for movement. Yes, you might have been busy all day running errands in your car or hammering away at your computer. This, unfortunately, doesn't count as movement. Physical activity is essential and no matter how many words you typed at work, you still need to get up and move.

Aim for Correct Standards

How do you measure whether you've been exercising enough? For most of us, it's looking at our predetermined routines and measuring ourselves against it. If we went to the gym 5 times this week, yes we've done it. If we lifted a certain amount of weight, it's legit and so on.

The problem with these standards is that they're all external. However, having internal standards, based purely upon how you feel, might be difficult at first. Therefore, it's a good idea to simply aim for at least 30 minutes worth of physical movement every day.

Note that I said movement, not intense strenuous exercise. You don't need to be doing HIIT or intense strength training just because you decide to do only 30 minutes of movement every day. Non-stressful activities like walking in the park, walking your dog, raking the leaves in your garden all count as physical activity.

You don't need to break a sweat every time you move in order for the movement to "count".

BUILD COMMITMENT

Aim to make exercise fun again. Remember how much fun you used to have as a kid running around at the playground? Well, that's what you need to aim for. You might not have the same level of abandon that kids have but you can certainly learn from them.

Kids don't think of exercise and movement as something to schedule. They just "do it". It's a natural state of being. This is what you need to remind yourself. You might have access to greater conveniences as an adult but that doesn't mean you need to sever your roots.

We were made to move, as human beings, and it's time you focus on how much fun and productive it can be. Make an extra effort to move more. For example, at work, climb a floor before taking the elevator. Try to increase this until you reach a comfortable level. Applying this sort of mindfulness prior to work is a great way to get yourself to focus immediately, instead of wasting time browsing the internet until you manage to get in the zone.

Always remember to listen to your body and respect its demand for rest and relaxation. It's perfectly fine to skip a workout if you're just too tired. This doesn't mean you veg out in front of the TV. Instead, do whatever you can and constantly check in with how you feel.

STEP 9- NOURISHING NUTRITION

This chapter is a tricky one for you to navigate and it requires you to really examine yourself prior to jumping in.

Thus far, I've been harping on about how there are no "bad" foods and that your decision to eat something should be based on whether you want to eat it or not. This "want to eat" is a combination of hunger and fullness signals (the degree of presence or absence of either) and whether you think you'll derive some pleasure out of it.

A natural question that arises from all this is: So when does the party stop? When are you going to tell me what exactly to eat?

INTUITIVE NUTRITION

First off, you will never hear an intuitive eater telling you what you should and should not eat. Intuitive eating is primarily based on listening to yourself and following what your body is telling you. This means if you want to go ahead and demolish that cheesecake, feel free to do so.

Isn't that bad for your health though? The calories alone would give you a heart attack! This is a good point and needs to be examined further before we get into the nutrition stuff.

Examine Yourself

That cheesecake that you just ate fully will affect your body in a certain way. At this juncture, ask yourself, how exactly are you thinking about these effects? Write them down on a piece of paper. Remember to include both the good and bad sides of it. Go ahead, I'll wait.

Once you're done, take a look at the language you're using to describe these good and bad qualities. Are you using words like "full of fat" or "too many calories"? Or are you using words like "will make me full past my limits" or "probably overeating" and so on? You could be using a mixture of both types of words. The idea is to get a grip on the kind of language you're using, not the proportion of the words.

Go Back or Move On?

Once you have an idea of how you're thinking about that cheesecake, it's time to evaluate what to do next. If your language shows that you still have a diet mentality, it's best to go back and reread all the chapters till now. Continuing on to read about nutrition will only harm you, since you will end up using the guidelines as rules. It's frustrating, yes, but it's for the best.

Examples of such language can be obvious like using words like "fat", "carbs", "calories", basing your thoughts on rules like "what time is it? Should I eat this after 5 PM?" or "How many veggies have I had? Have I earned this?" Take care to note not just your negative statements but positive ones as well.

Saying things like "I've earned this! I've suffered from diets for so long, I deserve this" or "Yeah I can eat this because it's tasty and comes under my total calorie requirement" is also a symptom of the diet mentality.

The intuitive way to think about this would be "I like the sound of it, I'll eat as much as I can or want" or "If I'm full after a meal, I really don't think I can eat an entire cheesecake" or "I'll have half my entree to go so that I can really indulge in that cheesecake" and so on. The decision to eat it or not is purely based on how you feel about it internally, not something external like calories, nutrients etc.

It's important for you to be honest here and take a long hard look at yourself. Again, it might be frustrating to go back and review everything but you'll do yourself a huge favor and increase the speed with which you become an intuitive eater by doing so.

Basics

While it isn't really important for you to know the ins and outs of all the macro and micronutrients, it's a good idea to know the basics about them. This serves dual purposes. First, it helps uninstall common statements you might have heard like "fat doesn't make you fat, sugar does" or "don't eat carbs after 6 PM" or "don't eat fruit if you wish to lose fat" and so on.

The important thing to understand about nutrition studies is that no matter the specific research being conducted, all studies usually point to the same thing, which is: all nutrients have a role to play. In excessive quantities, everything is bad for you. So eat everything in appropriate portions.

Carbs

We start off by looking at the most demonized of the lot, carbohydrates. Carbs have been demonized in mass media simply because they are essentially sugars. Sugar has become a swear word in nutrition circles, or fake nutrition circles I should say, so we've ended up with a bunch of nutty rules with regards to carbs.

Carbs are your body's primary fuel source. All carbs, essentially get broken down into sugars, usually glucose and fructose, and this is burned as fuel by your body to help you move around and do things that you do. This is heavily simplifying what actually goes on but it's a good summary and it's enough that you know this much.

Examples of foods that are carb heavy include grains, vegetables like potatoes, carrots, peas and things like pasta and fruit.

Protein

You and I and everyone else are pretty much the same when you reduce us down to our basic forms. We're all slabs of meat walking around. This is why you might have heard of proteins being referred to as "the building blocks of life". Proteins, broken down into their basic forms as amino acids, are what all meat is made of.

Given their nature, our bodies are extra smart when it comes to protein rationing. This once again reinforces the idea that our bodies need just a little help from us and they usually take care of the rest if we just get out of the way and go do whatever it is humans are supposed to do.

Protein regularly breaks down within our bodies but these broken down proteins are often "refurbished" and put to use once again in order to support our muscles. Therefore, it's not necessary to eat a huge amount of protein if you're a moderately active person. If you're extremely active physically, like an athlete or if you happen to lift boulders for 5 hours every day for some reason, you will need an extra dose of protein, around 1-1.5 grams ("How Much Protein To Build Muscle: What 51 Studies Say (2019 Update)")[1] per pound in body weight, to compensate for the increased breakdown.

Protein is usually found in greater quantities in meat such as beef, chicken, pork, and fish, but is also present in plants such as legumes and beans, and in dairy products like milk and cheese. There are small differences in the nature of these proteins but not enough to make it worth your while worrying about them. They're all good for you.

Fat

Yet another problematic macronutrient. As an aside, is it any wonder that diets fail when two out of three essential nutrients are basically ostracized by diets out there? No wonder, you're miserable when you follow one! Fat has been making a comeback with new studies showing how it is actually necessary, but this is usually at the cost of carbs.

Here's the thing: Nutrition is not a zero-sum game. If one nutrient is good, it doesn't mean another must be bad. All of them are necessary, in the right portions. If you're wondering about what the right portions are, don't worry, we'll soon look at this.

Fats form a major part of our brains, over 60% ("The Human Brain")[2], and fat is what enhances the flavor of our food. This is why we cook our food in oil, which is a fat. Fat is not just a one trick pony though. Burning fat also helps maintain our internal core temperature which is essential to ensure our organs function. In addition to this, fat is a secondary fuel source for our body and gets burned when there is a lack of carbs in the system.

There are different types of fats but again, unless you plan on becoming a nutritionist, it really isn't worth going into what they are. Keep in mind, again, that the key to eating the correct amount of fat is to eat a balanced diet. That sounds like a bit of circular reasoning but I'll explain it shortly.

Fats are found in foods like oil, lard, cheese, red meat, avocado and a variety of butters.

Micro Nutrients

If protein, carbs and fat are the heavy hitters, then vitamins and minerals are the consistent and dependable bats of your nutrition team. They can't carry things by their lonesome but will always be there to provide support.

In what is a chicken and egg evolutionary situation, our bodies are extremely smart when it comes to handling our stock of vitamins and minerals because they aren't as essential. Or perhaps they're non-essential which is why it's easier for our body to be smart about them?

The answer to that doesn't really matter and I've mentioned it just to illustrate that evolution has got us covered in ways we cannot even comprehend so we just need to provide our body some conscious backup support and the rest gets taken care of.

The major sources of vitamins and minerals are vegetables and fruits. Meat also has essential minerals which help bodily function. Calcium, which is necessary for healthy bone function, is perhaps the one mineral you should pay attention to with regards to intake. Dairy is a great source of this.

Having said all this though, the best way to get your dose of vitamins is to simply eat a balanced diet.

WHAT TO EAT

This is going to be a very short section since intuitive eating is not a diet. Remember, you already know, through your body and mind, what it is you need to eat. These guidelines will simply put you on the path to listen better.

- Eat a bunch of fruits and veggies- As a rough guideline, fill half your plate with some fruit or vegetables. It's not important what they are exactly, just eat a variety of them. So eat carrots one day, greens the next, apples and greens the next and so on.

- Make carbs your base- So rice, bread etc. should form the base of all your meals. Choose wholegrain when possible but it's not absolutely necessary. Your body will tell you what it wants if you listen. We'll look more into this in the next section but for now, regular pasta is just as good as whole grain.

- Get your protein- Have protein with every meal either as meat or through legumes.

- Get your Calcium- This is via dairy. So have a little cheese or milk. Yogurt is another option.

- Drink water- Water should be your primary fluid of choice. We all like some booze and fizzy drinks, yes, but remember to drink lots of water. 6-8 glasses at least.

- Include some nuts- Nuts are a great source of fat.

Butter also falls into this category. Your food will already have fat in the form of oil used in cooking so you don't need too much. A handful of nuts should do.

- Comfort and fun food- Chocolate, junk food etc belong here. Have a little every day if you want. Listen to your body and it will tell you when too much is too much.

- Fizzy drinks, filler foods- Minimize this as much as you can. There's no need to avoid them if you want it though. Take care that your water consumption is far greater than these.

That's it! Make sure you eat a portion of all the bullet points throughout the day. The points up till water are the major ones which tackle the macro nutrients. The remaining ones are aimed at filling gaps in micro nutrients and to satiate your comfort food cravings.

How Much to Eat

This is also going to be a short section. Usually what to eat and portion sizing are at the core of any diet plan. It's important to remember that intuitive eating is NOT a diet plan. Its aim is to get you to listen to your body and act accordingly because it knows what it needs the best.

Portion sizing will automatically take care of itself thanks to your body's internal mechanism. Think of it this way: How did you feel when you craved ice cream and ate multiple scoops of it? Did you feel the need to keep eating more? Or did your brain suddenly tell you that ice cream wasn't enjoyable anymore?

Once you start listening to your body, you'll find yourself making healthier choices to offset the unhealthy ones. This is why it's OK to have some junk or comfort food every day because your mind needs the pleasure it derives from food. At first, this will be a bit difficult to determine exactly but by following the guidelines above, you'll open your communication channels and will find yourself eating healthy naturally, as you're meant to.

I'm Vegan!

While a balanced diet is important, what is more important is to listen to your body. If eating meat or animal products makes you ill or just feels bad, then don't eat them. It's perfectly OK.

If you choose to adopt veganism as some sort of a dietary rule or philosophy of life then you're probably going down the wrong path since this is just another way of demonizing a particular food group and classifying it as good versus bad.

I Ate Too Much!

Yes. You did. Big deal. You will overeat sometimes and you will make mistakes. You will fumble around with portion sizes and eat too much or too little on certain days. You will eat too much ice cream and feel guilty and feel like you aren't capable of following this whole intuitive eating thing.

Relax. Take a few breaths. It's OK. Now remind yourself that this is normal and get back to listening and monitoring yourself.

CONCLUSION

Well, you've made it to the end. However, this is just the beginning. In essence, the preceding chapters were all about the end. The end of diet culture and the end of self-torture using food.

There are a number of things these days we use to torment ourselves. While addressing all of them is beyond the scope of this book, food and nutrition is something which you need not torment yourself with.

This self-torture stops now and it's time to love yourself and treat yourself the way you were meant to always do.

Join Heather's Facebook Group

@www.facebook.com/groups/PermittedFruit

Follow Heather on Instagram

@Permitted.Fruit

We hope you enjoyed this Plentifold production of Healing Intuitive Eating Transformation.

If you feel like sharing your thoughts on this book, we kindly ask you to leave a review on Amazon or Audible. It would help us spread the word and help more people. Thank You!

DISCLAIMER

This Book Does Not Provide Medical Advice

The information, including but not limited to, text, graphics, images and other material contained in this book are for informational purposes only. The purpose of this book is to promote broad consumer understanding and knowledge of various health topics. It is not intended to be a substitute for professional medical advice, diagnosis or treatment. Always seek the advice of your physician or other qualified health care provider with any questions you may have regarding a medical condition or treatment and before undertaking a health care regimen, and never disregard professional medical advice or delay in seeking it because of something you have read in this book. The author is not a [or your] health care provider. The author and publisher are providing this book and its contents on an "as is" basis and make no representations or warranties of any kind with respect to this book or its contents. The author and publisher disclaim all such representations and warranties, including for example warranties of merchantability and health care for a particular purpose. In addition, the author and publisher do not represent or warrant that the information accessible via this book is accurate, complete or current. The statements made about products and services have not been evaluated by the U.S. Food and Drug Administration. They are not intended to diagnose, treat, cure, or prevent any condition or disease. Please consult with your own physician or health care specialist regarding the suggestions and recommendations made in this book. Except as specifically stated in this book, neither the author or publisher, nor any authors, contributors, or other representatives will be liable for damages arising out of or in connection with the use of this book. This is a comprehensive limitation of liability that applies to all damages of any kind, including (without limitation) compensatory; direct, indirect or consequential damages; loss of data, income or profit; loss of or damage to property and claims of third parties. You understand that this book is not intended as a substitute for consultation with a licensed health care practitioner, such as your physician. This book provides content related to physical and/or mental health issues. As such, use of this book implies your acceptance of this disclaimer.

Made in the USA
Middletown, DE
22 July 2019